# Princesse de Clèves

# Princesse de Clèves

## Collected Works Volume 8

### John Watson

PUNCHER & WATTMANN

First published in 2023
Published by Puncher & Wattmann
PO Box 279
Waratah NSW 2298

info@puncherandwattmann.com

NATIONAL
LIBRARY
OF AUSTRALIA

A catologue record for this book is available from The National Library of Australia.

ISBN     9781922571656

Cover design by David Musgrave

Printed by Lightning Source International

*Verses based on the 1678 novel by*
*Madame de Lafayette*

*These verses follow the excellent translation by Terence Cave (Oxford, 1992).*

*i.m. William Maidment, Emblemist*

Never in the history of France
Was such display
                    and such a balance set
Between excess and reticence.

This was a time when the sun stood like a flower,
Its petals individual,
And turned its face towards the court
To shine in fond particularity
On games and fêtes and plays and tournaments.
In all of these the King was passionate:
The colours of Diane de Poitiers
Were in the field, her monogram,
Two D's enlaced, shared prominence
Beside the Queen's (who thus ensured
Her lasting closeness to the King).

Just as a flight of birds may in their pause
Appear to constellate and so denote
Configurations of significance
So, round the King stood dazzling galaxies:
The Queen and all her shimmering court;
Diane de Poitiers (Duchesse de Valentinois),
Their two bright stars fixed on opposing cusps;
Mlle de Marck, her grand-daughter;
Mme Elizabeth de France;
Marie Stuart, Queen of Scots
(There known as the Reine Dauphine);
The Duc de Guise;  the Chevalier de Guise;
The Vidame de Chartres;  the Cardinal de Lorraine;
The Duc de Nevers; his son the Prince de Clèves,
As charming as he was honourable;
The Maréchal de Saint-André,
And many others in this firmament

Including where the light seemed most intense,
The Duc de Nemours.

Few ladies at the court could not have wished
To see him at their feet, and few,
So finding him, could have resisted long.
Yet being kind as well as amorous
He could not, it was said, deny the sighs
Of those who sought to please him. Thus he had
At any time, a flush of mistresses.
But it was not known whom he loved.

There now appeared at court, startling yet calm
As a comet moving on a field of stars,
A young woman so entirely beautiful
That all eyes followed her.

The niece of the Vidame de Chartres,
She had been, following her father's death,
Raised lovingly by Mme de Chartres,
A lady of great wealth and virtue, who,
Devoted to her daughter, spent those years
In educating her away from court.

She taught her everything of love,
Its raptures and its oceanic power,
Nothing dissembling, so as to impress
Upon her its true dangers. So she stressed
The force of insincerity in men,
Its sea-wall devastating strength,
And taught that tranquil virtue may require
The most extreme mistrust of one's own powers
In order not to lose the mantle
                              of home and husband.

The young woman, so entirely beautiful,
On entering her sixteenth year
Already had been sought in marriage.
Mme de Chartres, thinking almost no-one
Worthy of her daughter, brought her to court.

That day the Vidame came to see her
And found himself astonished by her beauty:
Before a tapestry which slightly stirred
In the window's air, she stood in muted light,
Her face white against this figured scene,
Her fair hair bright beside its distant woods.

The following day she visited a jeweller
(A Florentine whose house glowed like the court)
To match some stones. While she was in his rooms
And as she held a topaz to the light
The Prince de Clèves entered.
                            Taken aback
By such persisting, fleeting beauty
He could not hide his mute astonishment
Did she but blush,
                    so palpably
His admiration filled the room.

That evening at the apartments of Madame,
The sister of the king, M. de Clèves,
Greatly perplexed, was troubled by one thought,
Who might this person be?

At first his breathless account was met with doubt;
Madame said there were none like that at court.

Mme de Dampierre, her lady-in-waiting
And friend of Mme de Chartres, hearing this,
Approached and whispered to her. Then Madame
Turned back inviting him, with promises,
To visit her the following day.

The night passed like a forest road.
Madame called, "Come and see, M. de Clèves,
If I have kept my word. Let me present
Mlle de Chartres. Is she not the one?"

M. de Clèves addressed Mlle de Chartres,
And begged her to remember it was he
Who first admired her and felt for her
The esteem which she deserved.

He left, that evening, with his friend,
The Chevalier de Guise.
                              Each had a secret;
They could not now converse with quite the same
Degree of warmth and openness. Each found,
Like moonlight breaking through a muslin cloud
Across a dark haphazard sea, that he
Was suddenly in love.

Mme de Chartres told her daughter:
"Never trust appearances at court.
What seems so, must be otherwise."

The ladies of the court (she said) compete
Like pleasure craft below a weir. They turn
As every current moves them variously.
Factions have crossed, passed closely and, at times,
Collided: those of the Reine Dauphine, the Queen,

And, vying with these, Mme de Valentinois;
With each collision fresh intrigues begin.

Mme de Chartres sought in this eddying pool
A husband for her daughter. But, at court,
As fountain plumes moved sideways in the breeze
And hulls were sometimes even found upturned,
The rapids forced her often from her course.

But into this congestion came a calm.
The Duc de Nevers died suddenly. His son,
The Prince de Clèves,
                                    after an interval
Of mourning, now felt free
To see Mlle de Chartres as his wife.

The Chevalier de Guise was not at court;
Others were, for a time,
Distracted by a maze of loyalties
For or against the Queen.
                                    The Prince de Clèves
Alone contrived to speak to Mlle de Chartres
Of love; he begged her to make clear to him
The  nature of her feelings — for his own
Were such that he would be eternally
Unhappy were she to marry him
From duty alone.

Mlle de Chartres felt some gratitude
For the Prince's courtesy, and this conferred
On all she said a gentleness
Which, with the billowing sail of beauty,
Allowed the Prince to entertain false hopes.
Mlle de Chartres spoke of what had passed.

Her mother said that there was little doubt
The Prince de Clèves was wise beyond his years,
Was kind, was admirable —
And should her daughter want to marry him,
She would most willingly consent.

The following day the Prince sent messengers
Conveying his proposal to Mme de Chartres,
Who, accepting it, felt no misgivings that
She was about to give
Her daughter to a man she could not love.

M. de Clèves found his was happiness
Without contentment. For he soon perceived
That Mlle de Chartres' sentiments
Were limited to gratitude and esteem,
And between the currents of their feelings lay
A barren reef.

"Can it be possible," he said,
"That I should be about to marry you,
The paragon desired by every man,
And not be happy? Yet it is true.
You feel for me only a form
Of kindness which could never be enough
To satisfy my love. For you are not
Impatient, restless or disturbed
By my anxious joy."

She said, "I do not know
What more you could expect of me. Would not
Decorum argue such constraint?"

"Alas, it is decorum which encourages
Your generosities. Behind these there is nothing,
Nothing of ardour, nothing to restrain."

"And yet," she said, "you cannot doubt
That I am glad to see you. You must see
How often in your company I blush."

Mlle de Chartres could not understand
These fine distinctions; and the Prince knew well
How far she was from feeling as he did.

The Chevalier de Guise returned too late.
The wedding was already imminent
And so he felt a grief as palpable
As it was futile. Faced with her loss
And in the presence of its pale
Wide-eyed embodiment, he could not speak.
Mlle de Chartres felt for him
Pity (but nothing more)
And told her mother of his courtesy.
Her mother judged too that her daughter felt
No more than sympathy for the Prince de Clèves.

The wedding party filled the Louvre.
The King took supper there with all the court;
Then in the apartments of Mme de Chartres,
The Chevalier de Guise could not conceal his grief.

M. de Clèves at no time thought
That when she took his name his wife had changed.
And so it was that, even as her husband,
He still remained her lover, since desire
Was unassuaged by mere possession. Thus

He was not happy. Restless passion raged,
Corroding his delight.
                                    Yet jealousy
Played no part in his suffering;
No husband had been further from its toils,
No wife from causing it.


Meanwhile the Duc de Nemours in Brussels
Was occupied with plans which soon should see
Him suitor to the young Queen of England.


He interrupted these elaborate plans
To come to Paris for the marriage of
The Duc de Lorraine.


Mme de Clèves spent all that day
Preparing for the ball. When she arrived,
Her beauty and the brilliance of her costume
Caused wonderment.


The ball began.
As she was dancing with M. de Guise
There was a noise. As all eyes turned
Towards the arrival at the ballroom doors
The dancing ended. Mme de Clèves now turned
To find her partner, but the King called to her
To take the person who had just arrived.
She turned and saw a man — M. de Nemours —
Stepping over a chair to make his way
On to the floor. He had such presence,
It would be difficult not to be taken aback
On seeing him for the first time, as difficult
As to see Mme de Clèves without amazement.

As they began to dance
Approving murmurs sounded in the hall
Like pebbles turning in a stream.

The Queen remarked how strange it seemed
To see this couple dancing in the brilliant light
Who did not know each other's name.

The ball continued; later, the Duc de Nemours
Danced with the Reine Dauphine who was
A woman of great beauty. Yet
His eyes sought everywhere Mme de Clèves.

The Chevalier de Guise who loved her still
Saw something in her face which troubled him.

Mme de Clèves came home,
Her mind so overflowing with the brilliant light
Of all that had happened at the ball
That she went, despite the hour, to her mother's room.
Mme de Chartres soon entertained
The same misgivings as the Chevalier de Guise.

During the following days
The Duc de Nemours seemed everywhere. Each door
Seemed to disclose him, framed in his own light;
She saw him with the Reine Dauphine
And everywhere he seemed to outshine
All others with his bearing, charm and wit.

Diane de Poitiers was always seen
At every fête and ball. Mme de Clèves
Was puzzled and often spoke of it.
She said to Mme de Chartres: "How is it that

The King has been so long in love with her
Who was his father's mistress and is still
The mistress of many others, yet
Has seen her grand-daughter married?"

"Ah, Madame de Valentinois!" said Mme de Chartres,
"Were I not afraid that you might think in me
What many say of women of my age,
That they delight in nothing more
Than telling endless stories of their day,
I would explain the complex origin
Of the King's long passion for Diane de Poitiers."

Her daughter begged her to begin.
"I am so ignorant still of all the intrigues
At court. There is so much I need to know."
Her mother traced the path to power
Of Diane de Poitiers; her noble birth;
Her beauty celebrated in the court;
Her rescue of her father from the scaffold;
Her liaison with the former King;
Her rivalry with the Duchesse d'Etampes
Over that King; her dazzling of his son,
The present King;
                        and in this nexus, high
Political intrigue born and sustained
By that rivalry.

Her mother stressed that passion's hidden face
Is always power, hearts are like coiled springs
Which drive the hands of fate. "In short," she said,
"Nothing is as it seems, and passion fuels
Events which seem remote from it."
His passion for Mme de Clèves

Now drove the Duc de Nemours towards extremes.
Of all the women he had loved
All others were erased from past and present.

The Reine Dauphine, once championed ardently,
Faded like flowers beside Mme de Clèves.
He only sought her company now
Because Mme de Clèves was often there.

And yet she seemed to him so rare a prize
He thought to tell her nothing of his passion
Lest public knowledge threaten it.
He did not even tell the Vidame de Chartres
From whom he normally hid nothing.
Only the Chevalier de Guise suspected him.

Mme de Clèves
                    felt something start away from her
And move towards him like a swing.

She mentioned to her mother every man
Who was in love with her
                         except one man,
Which absence troubled Mme de Chartres. Soon
An incident confirmed these fears.

One evening when the Reine Dauphine
Had called some favoured ladies to her room
To look at jewellery before the ball
The Maréchal was soon to give,
                      Mme de Clèves
Heard the opinions of the Duc de Nemours
Reported by a friend.
                         The Prince de Condé smiled:

"He says that no man likes to see
His mistress at a ball. For there, he says,
She dresses for all men, not just the man
Who loves her; and, excluded by her gaze,
He fears her beauty kindling other loves.
He says that there is only one thing worse
Than seeing his own mistress at a ball
And that is knowing she is there when he
Is absent unavoidably."
                    Mme de Clèves
Recalled that she had heard the Duc de Nemours
Could not be present at the Maréchal's ball.
She had no doubts that she was in his thoughts.

"He does allow," the Prince de Condé said,
"A man may like his mistress to attend
A ball he gives himself. For then
She flatters him in welcoming his guests."

The Reine Dauphine laughed. "He is right
To approve his mistress then — for otherwise
So many ladies would be kept at home,
There would be scarcely any women there."

Mme de Clèves felt suddenly
That she should not attend this latest ball.

She took the jewels chosen for her — but
Resolved that, since the Maréchal
Loudly declared his feelings for her, she
Should not attend.
                    Mme de Chartres,
Believing this decision mere caprice,
At length agreed, but said that she must feign

Some illness as a pretext. Mme de Clèves
Complied, and willingly remained at home
So as to avoid a place where M. de Nemours
Would not be present.

M. de Nemours returned. The following day
Mme de Chartres and Mme de Clèves
Were visiting the Reine Dauphine.

                                          She said,
"Princess, you look so beautiful,
I cannot believe that you were ill. I think
That, when you heard the Prince de Condé speak
Of M. de Nemours' opinion, then you thought
You would be obliging the Maréchal
(Who, everyone knows, is in love with you)
By not going to his house — and that is why
You did not attend the ball."

Mme de Clèves blushed
Because this was so near the truth,
And because M. de Nemours heard every word.

Mme de Chartres heard and understood.

Mme de Chartres waited several days
To speak of M. de Nemours. Then, casually,
She began to talk of him and, praising him,
Supplied as well the poisoned compliments
That in his wisdom he avoided love
With all its risks of pain. Instead (she said)
He chose a life of pleasure —
"There is of course his passion for
The Reine Dauphine. That has been seen as serious,
But still he keeps his freedom.

Mme de Clèves had never heard
These two names linked. She was greatly surprised
And thought that now she saw how grievously
Mistaken she had been about his feelings.
Mme de Chartres watched her brilliance fade.

She felt a sudden pang, discovering
What she already knew:
That her feelings for M. de Nemours were those
M. de Clèves expected for himself.

She held a dark bouquet of doubts.
                                                  She thought
Perhaps M. de Nemours was using her
In some way in his pursuit of the Reine Dauphine.

She intended to confess to Mme de Chartres
All that she had hidden.
But when the following day she went
To her mother's rooms to carry out this resolve
She found Mme de Chartres suffering
From a slight fever.
Thinking it better not to speak to her
She visited the Reine Dauphine.

"We were talking about M. de Nemours," she said,
"And were remarking with astonishment
How changed he is since visiting Brussels.
Before he went he had countless mistresses
But since his return he visits none of them."
Mme de Clèves did not reply, touched by
Some bitterness against the Reine Dauphine
Who seemed to feign astonishment when she
Must know the truth as well as anyone.

So, when the others left, she said
"Was it for me that you pretend surprise
When you yourself have caused this change of heart?"

"You are not fair," said the Reine Dauphine. "You know
That I hide nothing from you. Certainly
Before he went to Brussels, M. de Nemours
Admired me, yet on his return
He seems to remember nothing of the past.
But I shall find out what has touched his heart.
The Vidame de Chartres who is his friend
Is himself enamoured of a woman over whom
I have some influence…"

These words convinced Mme de Clèves.
Her state of mind was calmer than before.

When she returned, she found her mother ill,
Much more unwell than when she'd left.
Her fever increased and in the following days
Her daughter's anxious grief increased. She stayed
Almost continuously in her mother's room.
M. de Clèves, too, visited each day
Not only from respect for Mme de Chartres
But also for the pleasure which he found
In comforting his wife.
                         His passion had not waned.

M. de Nemours was similarly moved
To attend M. de Clèves to pay his regards
To Mme de Chartres in her illness. Sometimes
He called when M. de Clèves was absent. Then
He waited in Mme de Chartres' anteroom
With others — Mme de Clèves was often seen

Distraughtly pale but no less beautiful.

He spoke so gently and with such concern
For her distress that Mme de Clèves believed
It was not the Reine Dauphine whom he now loved.

Against her heavy counterweight of grief
She felt enchanted and disturbed.

Mme de Chartres sank into a shade
In which the sun
                    which briefly floods this world with light
Was scarcely present. The doctors now despaired,
While she showed fortitude and calm.
                                        When they had gone
She called Mme de Clèves to her side.

"My daughter, we must part."  She held out her hand.
"The danger facing you makes worse the regret
With which I leave you. You are troubled by
An inclination for M. de Nemours.
I had noticed it; I did not wish to speak
For fear of making you aware of it.
But now you are already on the brink,
My dearest child, you will now have to make
Great efforts and do violence to yourself
To keep yourself from ruin and despair.
Remember what you owe to others and
To yourself. Reflect that you are at the point
Of losing everything I wished for you.
Be brave. Remove yourself from court. Persuade
Your husband that you long to go away.
And have no fear of harsh and difficult
Decisions — even if they seem at first

More frightening than anything you've known —
Which must be more benign than to embark
Upon the miseries of illicit love.
Were you to suffer such ignominy
I would embrace death joyfully
In order not to witness such a thing."

Mme de Clèves burst into tears.
She held her mother's hand.
Mme de Chartres, herself touched by the sight,
Said, "Let us say no more of this,"
And then, "farewell my child."

She turned away. Mme de Clèves left her.
She lived for two days longer. In her grief,
Mme de Clèves turned to her husband, who,
As soon as these events had passed
Took her away into the countryside,
Far from this place which must increase her grief.

The kindness of her husband in these days
When grief was  mixed with fear of M. de Nemours
Made her the more determined not to fail
In her duty to M. de Clèves. And so
She showed him more affection than before;
She saw in him a friend, and found that she
Did not want him to leave her.
                                                      Soon


M. de Nemours called on her.
But Mme de Clèves resolved to use her grief
As an excuse not to be seen.

Her husband was obliged to go to Paris
And on his return, Mme de Clèves seemed grave.
She said, "If, in my present state,
Some further mishap could increase my sorrow
It would be the death of Mme de Tournon.
That news I heard this morning. She had been
A woman of great modesty, a friend
Most worthy of respect."

Her husband said "You should not grieve
If grieving for her virtues."
                              "You astonish me,"
Replied Mme de Clèves. "I've heard you say
No woman was more virtuous at court."
"Yes. That is true. But women are
Incomprehensible. And for that reason, I
Believe myself the most fortunate of  men
To have you as my wife."

"Your high regard is more than I deserve.
It is too soon to say that I
Am worthy of you.
                        But I beg you — please —
What disabused you of Mme de Tournon?"

"For some time now I've known
That she roused the hopes of the Comte de Sancerre.
But, if you wish, I'll tell you everything.

Two years ago, this mystery began.
I had not seen Sancerre for several weeks
And when we met I was surprised to find,
By accident, that although we are close friends,
He had concealed

His feelings for the widowed Madame de Tournon.

It happened in this way:  that evening
Before a play, we waited at the Louvre
For the King and Mme de Valentinois.
The King did not arrive and it was thought
The two had quarrelled as they often did
About the Maréchal de Brissac.
                                        Just then
M. d'Anville arrived and whispered to me
The King was in a state of great distress:
He had just found that Mme de Valentinois
Had given to the Maréchal a ring
Which he, the King, had given to her.
I told Sancerre but no-one else,
(As d'Anville had insisted). Yet, the next day,
I visited my mother-in-law and found
Mme de Tournon there. I was surprised
To hear from her this same account
And in the very words I'd told Sancerre
Who it was clear had visited her
That night, after the play —
All this while she was still professing grief
And wearing mourning dress.

Sancerre then told me of his ardent hopes
To marry Madame de Tournon!

Soon afterwards she did begin
To leave her solitary life. But, from that time,
Sancerre began to speak of doubts, as if,
Despite his undiminished passion, she
Had cooled towards him.

I tried to comfort him. I said
That if she lacked the strength to marry him
(Her reputation would be compromised)
Or if she loved another man, he must
Be patient and continue to regard
Her with respect and gratitude.

'This is,' I said, 'the advice which I myself
Would take. Because sincerity is all,
And if my mistress or my wife confessed to me
That she now loved another man, I would,
While feeling pain, endeavour to avoid
All bitterness and offer her compassion.' "

These words disquieted Mme de Clèves
And made her blush. M. de Clèves went on:

"Sancerre spoke openly to Mme de Tournon
But she assured him so convincingly
That for a period all his doubts were effaced.

But, nonetheless, she did defer
Their marriage until his return — for now
He was to take a journey for the King.
All this was several months ago.
Then, yesterday, I heard that she had died.
Sancerre returned that very day
And never have I seen a grief
So tender, so profound.

He said that he had rarely heard from her
During his absence, yet he knew
That letters could expose her to much risk;
He had no doubt she would have married him;

She was, he cried, the most deserving, true
And virtuous creature who had ever lived.

That afternoon I saw Sancerre again.
How changed he was!  Instead of tears,
He shook with furious rage.
He said, 'I have just heard
Something about Mme de Tournon
Worse than her death.'

I thought that grief had quite unhinged his mind.

'Mme de Tournon was unfaithful to me.
I am as much pained by her death as if
She had been faithful,
                                    and
As wounded by her infidelity
As if she were not dead.'

He told me how a friend — Estouteville, on
The very eve of her death, had come
In search of solace, unaware
Sancerre was suffering a similar grief.
It soon emerged that Estouteville fell in love
At just that time Sancerre had felt
Some faltering in her love for him.
Now Sancerre had to endure these words from him,
'I had the honour to console
Mme de Tournon after her husband's death.'

Sancerre went on
'At first I doubted him.
I went beyond the limits which a friend
Might normally recognise. I questioned him,

I pressed. At last he asked me if I knew
The lady's hand, and drew out with a sigh
Four letters and her portrait.
                              Ah! What letters,
What bitter fragrance and what tenderness,
What searing gentleness, which I
Had never known from her.

How happy yesterday I was in grief.
How wretched now that grief cannot remove
All that was thought to be but was not so.'

And when I left him to return to you
M. de Sancerre was still inconsolable."

Mme de Clèves expressed surprise.
"I had believed Mme de Tournon incapable
Of love and deception."

"I must return to visit the wretched man.
I think you must return to Paris too
For visits of condolence, which
Are as proper as they are unavoidable."

His wife agreed. About M. de Nemours
She was as calm as she had been for weeks;
Her mother's words, her own bereavement — all
Conspired to mute her feelings. Hence
She wrongly thought them totally dispelled.

The Reine Dauphine offered condolences,
Then told Mme de Clèves all that had passed
During her absence from the court.
"Of all events, the most remarkable

Is this:  M. de Nemours is passionately
In love — yet no-one knows with whom.
But certainly he is in love.
The Queen of England waits for him and still
He delays that journey. Now the King in jest
Suggests that he will have to send
Ambassadors to wed the Queen for him.
M. le Vidame is puzzled, for, although
He clearly is enthralled by some new love,
M. de Nemours is never out of sight
And keeps no assignations. Thus it seems —
Incredibly — an unrequited love."

Had Mme la Dauphine glanced at her
She must have seen Mme de Clève's distress,
To know herself to be the one
Whom no-one could identify, the one
For whom he turned aside the English crown.

But the Reine Dauphine suspected nothing.
"M. d'Anville from whom I gained this news
Insists that it is I who cause this change
And yet I should confess it were it so.
The woman who ignites such flames must sense
Their heat, and I detect in him only
A distance and distraction in his gaze."

The Princess was reclining on her bed.
The day was hot. M. de Nemours
Delayed his visit until other guests
Had left. The sight of M. de Nemours
Brought to her cheeks a flush which in no way
Distracted from her beauty.
                              Hesitant,

He sat and, for some time, said nothing.
At last he spoke, offering
His sympathy on her bereavement.
                                        Mme de Clèves,
Relieved to dwell on such a subject, spoke
Sadly about her loss.

Even when time, she said, had passed, she knew
That she would be altered irrevocably.

"Deep sorrows and extremes of passion,"
Replied M. de Nemours, "produce great change.
I hardly recognise myself
Since my return from Flanders. The Reine Dauphine
Remarked upon it only yesterday."

"Yes, it is so," said Mme de Clèves. "I seem
To recollect her speaking of it."

M. de Nemours now spoke at length:
"Madame, I am not sorry that she knows.
But there are others too who, I might wish,
Were as aware of it. There are some women
To whom we dare not speak of passion;
And yet we long for them to know
That every other woman in the world
Arouses in us mere indifference.
For what distinguishes a genuine
Attachment, in a clear, unwavering light,
Is to become the very opposite
Of all one was before, renouncing all
Pursuits and former pleasures."

Mme de Clèves well understood these words
As being like an arrow aimed at her.

She felt herself a target in a field.
She should reply yet not declare herself
In any way the object of these words.

She could not speak. She noted in these words
Both chivalry and something too precise
Not to offend her. Making no reply
She might by silence have seemed eloquent,
Had not M. de Clèves returned
And ended this exchange in pleasantries.

The prince had come to bring his wife
News of Sancerre.
                              She was so preoccupied
By what had taken place she could not hear.

She knew quite suddenly that she had been wrong
In trusting to professed indifference.

She could not any more delude herself
By hoping not to love him.
                              All she knew
Was that she must not give him any sign
Of her unbounded love. She must avoid
The presence of M. de Nemours.

Her state of mourning gave her the excuse:
She did not go to places where he might
Encounter her. She languished in a world
Of melancholy, and her mother's death
Could serve as the apparent cause.

So rarely did he see her now,
M. de Nemours despaired.
He knew he would not find her at the court
And could not bring himself to attend. Instead
He professed a passion for the hunt,
And so avoided gatherings where he knew
Her absence cast its shadow.
A minor illness for a time
Excused him from the court.

M. de Clèves too had been ill. His wife
Stayed with him but, as he grew well,
He sought out company once more
Including M. de Nemours.
                                                    She saw
That she must leave her husband's room
Whenever he was there, despite
The violence to herself which this required.

M. de Nemours now knew that she
Was avoiding him, and this discovery
Caused in him great regret mixed with delight.

Some days had passed. The King was visiting
The Queen's apartments where her circle gathered.
Conversation turned on horoscopes. The Queen
Spoke gravely of the science of prophecy.

The King was sceptical. "Some years ago
A noted seer came to the court.
I went with others, making them go first,
But the astrologer turned to me and prophesied
(Without perhaps quite knowing who I was)
That I should be killed in a duel. And, further,

That M. de Guise should die, killed from behind,
And d'Escard's head be struck by a horse's hoof.
We were displeased. As for myself,
The King of Spain and I have just made peace.
I hardly think it probable that I
Should take up duelling."
                              On this evidence
The company voiced disdain for all such science.

M. de Nemours said audibly, "I have
Less reason to believe in it than any man."
Then, turning to Mme de Clèves,
He added quietly, "I have been told
That I should be made happy by the love
Of one for whom I have a violent passion.
So, Madame, you may judge
If I ought to believe in prophecies."

"What are you whispering?" said the Reine Dauphine.

"Madame, I said that it had been foretold
That I should reach so elevated a station
That none might dare aspire to it."

"Well," said the Reine Dauphine, "if that were all
And with the rose of England in our thoughts,
You could have little reason to disdain
Such prophecies."

Mme de Clèves knew well
That M. de Nemours had not meant England.

Some time had now passed since her mother's death.
Mme de Clèves was seen again at court

And so she saw M. de Nemours once more
In the Reine Dauphine's apartments, and,
On his frequent visits to M. de Clèves,
Her agitation was discernible.

The English marriage and the frequent news
Of diplomatic moves towards that end,
The rumours of intransigence and doubt
Concerning this alliance in M. de Nemours
Engaged Mme de Clèves each day. And yet
She did not speak of it except to ask
About the beauty, wit and temperament
Of Queen Elizabeth. A portrait seemed
More striking than Mme de Clèves had wished.
She heard herself remark
That it perhaps was flattering to that Queen.

"I think not," said the Reine Dauphine.
"She is by reputation beautiful
As well as brilliant in debate. She has
Been held up as a model all my life.
Her qualities, of course, derive
From Anne Boleyn, her mother. I have heard
That Anne was animated in the extreme,
That she was most remarkable in being
Quite unlike every other English beauty."

Mme de Clèves said, "I have heard some say
That she was born in France."
"They were mistaken," said the Reine Dauphine.
"Briefly the facts are these:

She sprang from worthy English stock.
Henry VIII had been in love with both

Her sister and her mother. Some have thought
She was his daughter.

She came to France with Mary d'Angleterre,
A princess amorously inclined
(And sister of that English King).
Mistress Boleyn was said to be
As passionate as she. Here she acquired
An insight into court intrigues,
An interest in the new religion — and
French manners which on her return were found
A source of charm.
                              Susceptible, the King
Fell hopelessly in love with her
And so began his struggle with the Pope,

A conflict in which Church and state
Soon teetered on the pivot of his passion.

His Cardinal Wolsey as ambassador
Sought help in France. An interview, arranged
Between the Kings of France and England, saw
Competing gestures of magnificence.
Each offered clothing to the other, robes
Of crimson satin laced in diamonds, pearls
And gold. They met in Calais and Boulogne.

When Anne Boleyn was royally installed
In Henry's lodging with her retinue,
François I now treated her as Queen
And showered her with gifts. At last
The English King would wait no longer for
The Pope's consent and married her, and so
Declared himself the head of England's Church.

Despite the death of Catherine, Anne Boleyn
Did not enjoy her power for long. The king
Whose passion had enshrined her, soon fell prey
To jealousy. And one day as she watched,
With all the court, her brother Viscount Rochford
Tilting at the ring, the King abruptly left
And ordered her arrest and those he thought
— Through jealousy — to be her lovers.

The King in any case was now consumed
With feeling for Jane Seymour. Passion reigned,
And out of all control, within three weeks,
Had caused the death of Anne Boleyn."
Mme de Clèves was curious and asked
The Reine Dauphine to tell her even more
About the English Queen.

Mme La Dauphine had ordered miniatures
Of all the most beautiful women at the court;
And on the day on which Mme de Clèves
Was being painted she conversed with her.
The subject, pale and still, was watched also
By M. de Nemours who had not failed to come
As if by chance. She looked so beautiful
That had he not already loved her, he
Would not have failed to do so in this room.
He feared his feelings must be all too plain.

The Reine Dauphine had asked M. de Clèves
To bring a little portrait of his wife
In order to compare it with this one
Now almost finished. Everyone
Was eager to pass judgement. Mme de Clèves
Desired a detail added to the one

Already framed and, to this end,
The ivory was removed. The painter worked,
Adjusting the coiffure, then set it down.

M. de Nemours had long desired to have
A portrait of Mme de Clèves.
He judged that in this company
Suspicion would not fall on him.

Mme La Dauphine was sitting on the bed
And speaking to Mme de Clèves, who stood
Between the half drawn curtain and the room
Beyond whose windows trees were luminous.
She saw M. de Nemours
Move backwards and without a downward glance
Pick something up. She had no difficulty
In knowing what it was. She was disturbed.
The Reine Dauphine asked audibly what was
The matter. Hearing this,
M. de Nemours turned round and met the gaze
Of Mme de Clèves.

She was disturbed. She could not ask in public
For the portrait, since to do so would proclaim
His interest in her, while to ask in private
Would be to invite his heartfelt declaration.

By saying nothing she convinced herself
That she was granting this one favour
Without his knowing it.

M. de Nemours left suddenly. He felt
The perilous and uncontainable
Delight that he possessed

Her image. And she knew what he had done.
In his room he gazed at it:
This image breathed her knowledge. And he had seen
In her disquiet the innocence of love.

That evening, despite a thorough search,
The portrait was not found. Its open case
Suggested it had fallen and been lost.
M. de Clèves said jestingly that, perhaps,
She had a hidden lover who
Had stolen it or begged it from her hand.

Her husband's words spoken in jest, produced
Remorse caught like a veil of gauze across
The thorn bush of her passion. Now she saw
The violence which was drawing her towards
M. de Nemours.

She saw the abyss,
She thought of Mme de Chartres' parting words.
She felt the imminence of danger, being
Unable to dissemble, which would mean
M. de Nemours must see into her heart.

She remembered too her husband's words
About sincerity and Mme de Tournon.
It seemed to her that perhaps she should confess
To him her feelings.
                        This idea
Preoccupied her for some time; and then
She was astonished by it, and it seemed
Like madness.
                        Then she fell back once again
Into not knowing what to do.

But now two royal marriages were planned;
Elizabeth the daughter of the King
Agreed at last to wed the King of Spain,
Who would be represented on this day
In all his splendour by the Duc d'Albe;
And Marguerite, his sister, was engaged
To the Duc de Savoie. Both weddings would occur
On one illustrious surpassing day
Which would outshine the sun itself.

Elaborate plays and ballets were proposed.
The King envisaged something even more
Impressive, and announced a tournament
At which his foreign visitors could compete,
And all his loyal subjects could attend.
The King, the Duc de Ferrare, M. de Guise
And M. de Nemours would join to constitute
The four champions of the tournament.

Accordingly, advertisements appeared
Throughout the realm, announcing that
On June 15, in the city of Paris,
There was to be a tournament, at which
His Most Supreme and Christian Majesty
Together with the princes Alphonse d'Este,
The Duc de Ferrrare, François de Lorraine,
The Duc de Guise, Jacques de Savoie
And the Duc de Nemours, would challenge all comers.

The rules of contest were elaborate:
The first course to be combat in the lists
On horseback, four lances to be broken,
A fifth in honour of the ladies;
The second to be fought with swords, in pairs

Or singly as the marshals should decree;
The third on foot with three thrusts of the pike
And six with swords; strict penalties to apply
To a rider striking his opponent's horse;
Determinations touching house and rank
To be proclaimed three days before the lists;
The rules concerning shields most delicate;
Devices, colours amorous, coats of arms,
To be noted by an officer-at-arms;
Numbers of lances broken or swords crossed
To be recorded for the award of prizes.

A splendid field of combat was declared
Extending from the Château des Tournelles,
Crossing the Rue Saint Antoine,
And ending at the royal stables.

Wooden stands and covered banks of seats
Were set up on both sides.
Bright canopies were raised. Pavilions, groves,
Flammarions, billowing silks
Were all in readiness for the tournament.

And while the flowering field was being raised
The King played tennis with the Vidame de Chartres,
M. de Nemours and the Chevalier de Guise.
The ladies of the court looked on.
And when the game was over, Chastelart
Approached the Reine Dauphine and said that chance

Had now directed to his hand a letter
Fallen from M. de Nemours' pocket.

She took it and, accompanying the Queen,
Set out to watch the furnishing of the field.

The lists were well advanced. The King brought out
Some horses, partly broken in, to test,
Presenting one to each of his companions.
By chance the King and M. de Nemours
Now found themselves on headstrong mounts. The King
Reined in his horse. It reared, and M. de Nemours,
In order to protect the King, backed off
Abruptly. As he turned, his mount struck out,
Colliding with a pillar of the lists
So violently M. de Nemours was flung
Against the wall.
                    People ran to him.
Mme de Clèves was so alarmed
She could not think of hiding her dismay.

And the Chevalier de Guise watched her
With greater interest than he paid
The dazed M. de Nemours,

Who now rose slowly. As he stirred
He saw the image of Mme de Clèves
Bent over him,
Her face pale with distress.

She saw him recognise her own concern.

M. de Nemours was dazed, but thanked the Queen
And all her ladies for their kindness.

The King then ordered him to go and rest.

The Chevalier de Guise, disturbed
By what he'd seen, approached Mme de Clèves.
He walked with her back from the lists.
He said,

       "Madame, I am more to pity
Than M. de Nemours. My faint hopes
Have vanished. For I have just lost
The meagre consolation of belief
That all who dare to gaze on you are as
Unfortunate as I, and languish too.

This is the first and last time I will speak.
I see that there is hope, and none for me."

He murmured as they walked
That only death or exile now could end
The torment of this place. He would, he said,
Seek some great enterprise; he had, in fact,
For some time, entertained the thought
Of taking Rhodes for France. He was resolved…

Mme de Clèves could only hesitate,
Pretending puzzlement. But now she feared
The whole world must have seen and read her thoughts.

While calling on the Queen, Mme de Clèves
Was much preoccupied.
M. de Nemours arrived soon afterwards
Magnificently dressed and quite unhurt.
The King, emerging from an ante-room
And summoning him to ask if he were well,
Gave him this opportunity to speak
To Mme de Clèves in passing her:  "Madame,
Today you showed me pity. This alone

Is not all I deserve."

                Mme de Clèves
Was pained to have confirmed that she had shown
So much that she should hide. And yet this pain
Was curiously sweet.

Mme la Dauphine, impatient to discuss
The contents of the letter,
Approached Mme de Clèves. "Go quickly. Read
This letter to M. de Nemours. Then come
This evening to my *coucher* and tell me if
You know the hand."

She went immediately to her private room,
Although this was not her appointed hour
To withdraw. She trembled as she read.

        "For too long I have loved you too much to allow
        The changes you observe in me
        To be explained by my inconstancy; they are
        In fact, the consequences of
        Your infidelity which you had hidden well,
        So well that you had every cause
        To be astonished at my knowledge of its cause.
        Nothing can match the pain I feel.
        I thought that you were violently in love with me;
        I ceased to hide my passion. Then
        Precisely as I cast off all my last reserve
        I learnt that you were deceiving me.
        It was the morning of the tilting at the ring
        And that is why I stayed away,
        Feigning an illness to conceal my true confusion.
        But with this violent distress
        My body made that phantom illness actual.

I suffered. Then, recovering,
I gave myself more time by feigning illness still
And thought of what to do. At last
It came to me that I should feign also decline
In my affections, which must seem
Diminished of their own accord and not because
Of any treachery of yours.
The woman you now chose must not feel flattered by
My knowledge of her victory.
I realized that you must love me still, if my
Withdrawal were to cause its wound;
I had to seem to love you less yet still pretend
To keep the fact from you. What pain
This path between two seeming truths caused me!
And yet I did succeed. In time
I knew that your perversity had this effect,
That as you saw me move away
You loved me more, perhaps, than you had ever done.
I thought that you had given up
The one for whom you had abandoned me ... And yet
I know that even at this time
You still continually deceived me without shame.
Do not pretend surprise that I
Must irrevocably refuse to speak to you."

Mme de Clèves read and re-read the letter
Without quite understanding it. She only knew
M. de Nemours was not in love with her
As she had thought,
            and that he loved others
Whom he deceived as he was deceiving her.

Had not M. de Nemours (she thought)
So clearly had good grounds to sense her love
When he was dazed and rising to his feet,
Still half caught by the horses' hooves —
Then she would not have cared at all
On finding that he loved another.
                                        But
(She knew) all this was self-deceit.
In fact, the pain she felt was jealousy
With all its demons.
                        She read the letter yet again.


She envied the capacity in its author
To hide her feelings from M. de Nemours.
The writer, too, she noted, had believed
He loved her. Might not his restraint which seemed
So touching be in part the result
Of passion for this other?


How painfully she heard her mother's words.
How she repented failing to insist,
Despite M. de Clèves,
That she should go far from society.


And she had failed
In her resolve to tell her husband all
She felt for M. de Nemours, and so rely
On his great kindness and his own concern
To keep such secrets from a man
Who was deceiving her as he deceived
The author of this letter.
Her only consolation was that now,
At least, she had no more to fear
From her own feelings for Nemours.

She quite forgot the Reine Dauphine.
The *coucher* scarcely crossed her mind. Instead,
Pretending she was indisposed, she went to bed.
M. de Clèves returning from the King
Was told that she was sleeping.

                           But she spent
A sleepless night, the letter in her hand.

Mme de Clèves was not the only one
Made sleepless by that letter:
The Vidame de Chartres —
For it was he and not M. de Nemours
Who lost the letter —
Was in a state of great anxiety.

That night at dinner he had found
The letter missing. Later, a valet of the Queen
Came to him, telling him it had been said
A letter fallen from his pocket was now
In Chastelart's possession.

Dismayed, the Vidame called on and roused,
Despite the hour, a gentleman who was
An intimate of Chastelart.
He begged him to set out at once to retrieve
This damning letter, telling Chastelart
Neither its owner nor who sent for it.

Since Chastelart already was convinced
The letter had been mislaid by Nemours
Who was — he thought — his rival for Mme la Dauphine
He took malicious pleasure in the fact
That he had passed the letter on to her.

Alarmed on hearing this, the Vidame thought
That only M. de Nemours could help him now.
A froth of daylight had begun to rise
Through M. de Nemours' bed-chamber when
The Vidame woke him.

                      He was surprised
And puzzled to be asked a curious favour:

"A letter which I should have guarded with
The utmost secrecy I lost.
It has been found. Already
Several people at the tennis court
Have seen it.

               As you were there,
I beg you to maintain that it was you
Who lost it."

"But surely —
If the letter is so dangerous
It must be so to me."

"Please listen seriously," said the Vidame.
"If you have a mistress — which I do not doubt —
There is a way for you to vindicate
Yourself despite the letter,

                     even if
At the expense of some brief quarrel —
Whereas I, unless you intervene, must bring
Disgrace upon a woman who deserves
Only esteem, and, on myself,
The most destructive hatred and perhaps
The loss of all my fortune."

"I have heard rumours," said Nemours, "but, still,
I do not fully understand."

"I see that I must tell you everything
And hope that you may see that what I seek
Is small enough compared with this calamity:

Two years ago, at Fontainebleu, the Queen
Began to speak of trust.
I said that there were certain things
Which I would trust to no-one. She seemed pleased.

She said that she had never found in France
A person worthy of her confidence.

She raised the matter several times again;
She even mentioned several delicate
And private matters — I think, a way
Of testing my discretion.
Flattered and troubled, I spent more time with her.

One evening, when the King and ladies rode
Into the woods, she said she felt unwell
And lingered near the lake. I stayed with her.
Dismissing her attendant, she began:

'I want to speak to you. You are in love,
And while you would believe that no-one knows,
This secret is in fact well known to some
Who watch you and your mistress. I do not know,
Nor ask you who she is. I only wish
To warn you.'
                    Now you see in this,
A stratagem. The Queen desired to know

If I were in love, but in this way maintained
Her own indifference.

Now while I loved Mme de Thémines
And, although she loved me too, we had as yet
Not found some private place in which to meet.
I knew therefore that something else must be
The source of this intelligence. I was
At this time in the throes of a love affair
With another woman much less beautiful
And less severe than Mme de Thémines.
With her, perhaps, my meetings had been seen.

I determined to admit nothing
To the Queen;
                rather, I would say
That I had long since given up the desire
To seek the love of other women, since
The true prize now was far above their level.
The Queen objected:  I was insincere.
She said, 'I should like you to be a friend.
But, if this were to be, then I would need
To know of your attachments and would view
Deception as beyond forgiveness.'

She asked me to consider all she'd said
For two days more. Of course, my vanity
Was flattered by the thought of entering on
A private understanding with the Queen;
And yet I loved Mme de Thémines;
Although I had been, in a sense,
Unfaithful I could not give up
All thoughts of her.

And so, reluctantly I broke
With the other woman, and I hoped
To keep my feelings for Mme de Thémines
A secret from the Queen.

Those two days passed. The Queen
Approached me as I walked amongst her ladies.
'And have you given thought,' she said
To all I charged you with, and do you have
An answer?'

'Yes, Madame,' I said,
'It is as I have told your Majesty.'

'Come then this evening,' she said, walking on,
'But I shall write to let you know the hour.'

I found her in her gallery. She said,
'Well! Did you need to think so long and hard
In order to decide to tell me nothing?
Have I not earned a more sincere response?'

.'It is because of my sincerity
That I have nothing to relate. I swear,
With all the respect I owe you, that I care
Nothing for any woman here at court.'

'I will believe you,' said the Queen
'Because I wish it to be so. It is
My desire that you should be exclusively
Attached to me. Were you in love, you would
Be unreliable, distracted, frail,
Uncertain in your loyalties. I want
Your undivided confidence, so that

I may entrust my sorrows to your care —
As you may guess they are not trivial;
It is supposed I happily accept
My husband's mistress here at court. In fact
It is intolerable, and causes me much pain.
Diane de Poitiers despises me
As much as she deceives the foolish King;
My people all are in her pay. And then,
My daughter-in-law, the Reine Dauphine, who is

Obsessed with being beautiful, obeys
The slightest whim but never thinks of me.'
The Queen went on, reciting other trials
Until tears gathered and would fall. She said,
'I place my trust in you. Do not betray
This trust, which will be absolute.'

But even occupied as I now was
So gratifyingly with the Queen (whose charms
Are still considerable) I could not still
My feelings for Mme de Thémines. And yet
It seemed, increasingly, her love for me
Was coming to an end and, had I been
More prudent, I would have withdrawn. Instead,
My passion for her now was doubly strong.
I was so clumsy that the Queen soon guessed
Something had changed. In women of her nation
Jealousy is natural. At once
I found that my protestations to the Queen
Required increasing repetition. These
Were aided by the strength of Mme de Thémines'
Rejection of me which at last enforced
My leaving her in peace. Eventually
She wrote to me the letter which I lost.

With my affections quelled elsewhere,
The Queen seemed more content.
                              But, perhaps, because
My feelings for her are not such as could
Prevent attractions elsewhere, and because
One cannot love at will, I have
Become enamoured of Mme de Martigues.


Because this lady visits frequently
The Reine Dauphine, I often go there too;
And now the Queen has seized on the idea
That it is she whom I love. The Queen
Is capable of jealousy almost
Approaching madness. The Cardinal of Lorraine,
Aspiring to her favour, makes things worse.


Imagine if you will the dire result
Should someone show my letter to the Queen.
Then she would know
That I not only had deceived her with
Mme de Thémines but at that same time was
Unfaithful to that lady with another. Then
There is Mme de Martigues…
                              So you see
How urgently I beg you to proclaim
The letter yours."


"It's clear to me," said M. de Nemours
"That you have been most irresponsible.
How could you think the Queen would not perceive
Your gross duplicity. Did you not know
The Queen is fiercely and possessively
In love with you? She is Italian!"

"Your own caprices should have made you more
Indulgent. Rather than reproach me now,
I hoped that you would take my side."

"But if the letter had been seen
To fall from your own pocket how can I
Convince them it is mine?"

"I thought you knew. The Reine Dauphine was told
That it was yours.
Your servants went with mine to fetch our clothes
From the tennis courts. The letter fell. Some thought
It came from my clothes, some thought yours."

M. de Nemours felt suddenly alarmed.
This made the option of pretence that he
Had lost the letter seem more dangerous.
He thought at once of Mme de Clèves.

The Vidame said, "It is obvious you fear
Recrimination from your mistress, should
You do as I have asked. But here
You see the remedy: This is a note
From Mme d'Amboise, a friend of Mme de Thémines,
Who asks on her friend's behalf that I return
The letter I have lost. Take this note
And show it to your mistress should you need
To prove the letter is not yours.
                              I beg you
Go to Mme la Dauphine."

M. de Nemours agreed. He took the note
But set out not to the Reine Dauphine
But to Mme de Clèves, who,

Sleepless in bed, was startled when his name
Was brought to her. Embittered, she refused
To see him, pleading illness.

M. de Nemours sought out M. de Clèves
In his apartment and explained
That he had wished to speak most urgently
To his wife concerning the Vidame de Chartres.
M. de Clèves, sensing this urgency,
Conducted him to her room.
                              She was confused,
But the darkness of her room helped her disguise
Her startlement. M. de Clèves explained
That his friend had something urgent to impart
About her uncle. Meanwhile he,
M. de Clèves, had business with the King
And left them to discuss
Some matter of a mislaid letter.

Dark curtains were drawn back. The light
Dawned in the room. He saw
Roses like faded silk. Mme de Clèves
Regarded him with bitterness and doubts.
He said, "Madame I came in haste to ask
About a certain letter — "

"I have heard something of this letter. But
I cannot see how it concerns my uncle.
He is not named in it."
                        "He is not, Madame,
And yet the letter is addressed to him,
And I assure you it is like a sword
Suspended over him, unless you go
To retrieve it from the Reine Dauphine."

"I find it hard to understand my rôle
In its retrieval," said Mme de Clèves,
"Since she believes it was addressed to you."

Her bitter tone and all that it implied
About her interest in the letter, filled
Him with such hopes as almost overcame
His need to vindicate himself. He said,

"The letter is not mine and if there is
One person I will see convinced of this,
It is not Mme la Dauphine.
                    But, Madame,
Allow me to explain the urgency
Of all this for your uncle."

Mme de Clèves was silent. M. de Nemours
Recounted to her all the Vidame had said.
She listened with a cold reserve until

The note for Mme d'Amboise persuaded her
Nemours was innocent of all intrigue.

She eagerly discussed her uncle's plight;
His conduct she condemned but was amazed
At his involvement with the Queen.
                         And now
She admitted that she had the letter, and
Began admitting all its contents which
So recently she had disdained.
                    They agreed
It would be better not
To give the letter to the Reine Dauphine
In case she showed it to Mme de Martigues.

They thought it wise also to say nothing
About the Queen. Mme de Clèves enjoyed
The sharing of these secrets.

M. de Nemours would perhaps have touched
On other matters,
                              had not Mme de Clèves
Been summoned by the Reine Dauphine.

As soon as she arrived Mme la Dauphine
Said in a low voice, "Never have I known
The truth so awkward to disguise —
The Queen has heard about the letter. She
Is sure it implicates the Vidame de Chartres
And is intent on seeing it. She thinks
— I'm sure — that I am in some way involved
With him. Give me the letter. Let the Queen
Discover what she will in it."
                              Embarrassed,
Mme de Clèves said, "I am at a loss
To know what should be done. For M. de Clèves
To whom I showed the letter has,
This morning, passed it on to M. de Nemours
Who came at first light for it."

"You had no right to deal so freely with it.
This places me in the most difficult
Position. What am I to say? The Queen
Will think the letter further evidence
Connecting the Vidame with me.
                              She will never
Be convinced the letter is M. de Nemours'."

"I am dismayed," replied Mme de Clèves,
At the embarrassment I've caused — and yet
The fault is M. de Clèves'."

"The fault lies in your giving him the letter;
You are the only woman in the world
Who tells her husband everything."

"No doubt I was remiss but should we not
Think only now of remedies?"

"Do you remember what was in the letter?"
"Yes, Madame, I read it several times."
"Well then," continued Mme la Dauphine, "you must
Immediately write it down from memory,
And in an unknown hand.
                    The Queen will not know."

Mme de Clèves assented — for she thought
M. de Nemours could bring the letter back
And they could copy it together.

She hastened home. M. de Nemours was summoned
And he came at once
                    but empty-handed:
He had already given the letter back
To the Vidame
            who, delighted, had
Sent it at once to Mme de Thémines' friend.

But this predicament was soon resolved
With eagerness. Mme de Clèves and M. de Nemours
Would write the letter out from memory.
They shut themselves away to work on it

With orders to the servants at the door
To admit no-one. This atmosphere,
Intensely secret and mysterious,
Held no small charm for both protagonists.
The presence of her husband in the house —
But in its outer shadows —
Allowed Mme de Clèves to silence all her scruples.

She felt only the pure, unmixed delight
At seeing M. de Nemours,
And from delight arose a gaiety
Which M. de Nemours had never seen in her,
And which increased his love beyond all measure.

He was therefore amusing and capricious.
Mme de Clèves was similarly moved
To frivolous light-heartedness so that
Their task proceeded intermittently.
By four o'clock the letter was complete
But unconvincing,
                    and the Queen,
When she examined it suspiciously,
Was not deceived. In fact she was not swayed
From her conclusion that the Vidame de Chartres
Had not only betrayed her but had shared
Some understanding with the Reine Dauphine.

This was to lead
To eventual ruin for the Vidame de Chartes,
His role as confidant to the Queen
Never resuming;
                    and for the Reine Dauphine
Increasing hatred, ending in her forced
Exile from France.

After the letter had been sent,
                    Mme de Clèves
Remained alone.
                    Sustained no longer by the joy
Of being with a person whom one loves
She woke as from a dream.
She contemplated with astonishment
The gulf between successive days.
                    She recalled
Her cold and bitter attitude to M. de Nemours
So recently, when she believed
The letter from Mme de Thémines was his,
And now how calm and gentle she had been
Towards him when he had persuaded her
The letter was not his.

And she reflected that, the previous day,
She had reproached herself, as if it were a crime,
For showing by her jealousy her true
Affection for him;
Now she could scarcely recognise herself.

For now, she thought, she had revealed the same
Immoderate passion by her afternoon with him
And therefore had deceived her husband who
Was least of all deserving of deceit.
She felt ashamed to seem, even in the eyes
Of M. de Nemours so unworthy of esteem.

But most of all she was distressed, remembering
The state in which she had passed the previous night
Believing him in love with another woman, and
Therefore unfaithful to her.
She had been ignorant of jealousy,

She had feared only weakness in herself,
That she might fall in love with M. de Nemours,
And had not yet begun to fear that he
Might ever love another.
                              Yet the letter,
Even as her doubts had been allayed,
Had made her painfully aware of doubt,
The possibility at least
Of deceit, distrust and jealousy.


She was astonished that she had not thought
A man like M. de Nemours,
Well known for superficiality
Regarding women, might be incapable
Of true sincerity. It might in fact
Be quite impossible to find in him
True happiness. "But even if I could,"
She thought, almost aloud,
                              "What can I want with it?
Do I desire to be unfaithful to
M. de Clèves and to myself?  Do I wish
The remorse and mortal suffering that love
Gives rise to?  I am overcome
By currents carrying me despite myself;
My resolutions are to no avail.
Today I felt as I did yesterday
Yet laughed as freely as, before, I had
Seemed bitter and reproachful."
                              She resolved
Again, that she must tear herself away
From M. de Nemours; she spent that evening
At home, not visiting the Reine Dauphine,
Not curious about the effects
Of the false letter.

When M. de Clèves returned,
She told him that she was unwell, she wished
To go into the countryside,
She needed fresh air, solitude and quiet.
She looked so beautiful,
M. de Clèves could not believe she was unwell.

At first he mocked the thought;
He gently asked was she forgetting
The wedding of the princesses
And then the tournament? For these, he thought,
She would need to prepare
To match the splendour of the other women.
But the weddings and the tournament, the blur
Of brilliances at court could not persuade
Mme de Clèves to change her mind.
She begged her husband to allow,
While he went to Compiègne with the King,
That she should go to Coulommiers, their house
Not yet completed, one day's carriage ride
From Paris.
          M. de Clèves gave his consent.

It had been difficult for M. de Nemours
After that afternoon to be deprived
Of even the least glimpse of Mme de Clèves.
The court seemed empty; every day was filled
With restless, grey impatience.
                    He resolved
To visit his sister, the Duchesse de Mercoeur
Whose house was not far from Coulommiers.
He asked the Vidame to go with him,
Already hopeful that with him he might
Soon call upon Mme de Clèves.

Mme de Mercoeur was pleased to see her brother;
She entertained them, offering them all
The many pleasures of the countryside.

While out stag-hunting, M. de Nemours
Became lost in the forest.
A shepherd told him he was very near
Coulommiers.
                    Hearing the name, without
A clear intention, he rode off at a gallop
Into the forest in the direction of
Coulommiers, and followed paths
He knew must lead him to the château.
                                        Soon
He reached a small pavilion.
                              Of three rooms,
The outer ones adjoined a flower maze
And a winding avenue into the park.

He had not reached the central room
When, from the window of the first, he saw
Mme de Clèves approaching with her husband.

He was surprised, for he had left M. de Clèves
In Paris with the King. Yet here they were,
Closer and walking down the avenue.

His instinct was to hide. He did not wish
To see M. de Clèves. But now they arrived
And, leaving several servants at the door,
Entered the outer room furthest from him
To sit alone in the larger, inner room.

M. de Nemours could not now leave
Without encountering the servants. He had,
He thought, no choice but to remain
And overhear her conversation with
Her husband who caused him more jealousy
Than any of his other rivals.

He listened just to hear her voice. He heard
M. de Clèves:
"But why are you determined not to come
With me to Paris? For some time you have
Sought solitude, and this distresses me
Because it keeps us far apart. I fear
That you are melancholy for some reason."

"I have nothing
Particularly disturbing on my mind
But while the court is crowded and so many
People visit us I find I long
For quiet and tranquillity."

"Tranquillity is not what I would think
A woman of your age needs most. My fear
Would rather be that you desired to be
Apart from me."

Increasingly embarrassed she replied:
"It would be most unjust if you thought that.
But I implore you to allow me time
To stay here. If you could remain,
But without company, I would welcome it."

"Madame," cried M. de Clèves, "I see you have
Some reasons to remain alone — of which

I am unaware. I beg you now
To tell me what they are."


He pressed her for her reasons and became,
As she resisted, still more curious.
She fell into a silence.
                    Then she said,
Looking at him as she had never done,


"Do not oblige me to confess
Something which I have not the strength to confess
Although I have considered it. Only believe
It is not prudent for a woman of my age
To be alone at court
                    Surrounded by
So many influences."


"What base conclusion would you lead me to?
I hesitate to think what you can mean."


Mme de Clèves made no reply.
And yet her silence made him think the worst.
"You still say nothing. Am I forced to think
Of abject possibilities?"


"Well then, Monsieur," she said,
Throwing herself at his feet, "I will make
A confession which no woman ever made
To her husband. Only my innocence gives me
The strength to make it. It is true
I have my reasons to withdraw from court
And to avoid the dangers which beset
All women of my age.
                    And yet I have

Shown not one sign of weakness, and would have
No fears were I to stay here far from court,
Or had Mme de Chartres with me still.

However dangerous my actions now,
I must persist and so retain the hope
Of being worthy of you as a wife.
I ask a thousand pardons if I have
Emotions which displease you. But at least
I will not ever shake your faith in me
By any actions.
                    But reflect
How great is my affectionate esteem
That I confide in you so openly."

Throughout this speech M. de Clèves had sat,
His head held in his hands.
He looked at her.
                    In tears
How strangely beautiful she was.

How tearful seemed the room, as if the air
Were pressed with pearls. Embracing her, he said,
"If I do not respond as you expect
Because of violent distress, forgive me.
No woman has been worthier in my eyes
And yet I am the unhappiest man
In the world. I loved you passionately
From the first, yet never have inspired in you
The love which agitates you now.

Who is he then, Madame, this happy man
Who makes you so afraid? How long have you
Been drawn to him? What means has he devised

To find a way into your heart? I am
Both envious husband and a jealous lover,
And yet I find some comfort in your trust,
And reassurance in sincerity,
Although unhappiness must flow from this
Proof of fidelity.
                    But, Madame,
You have not finished. Tell me who it is
You wish to avoid."


"I beg you not to ask me that," she said,
"For I believe that prudence must dictate
That I not name him."


"Have no such fear, Madame. I know the world
Too well to doubt that many men respect
The husband yet may find his wife
Entirely irresistible.
I may not hate such a man and yet avoid
Public complaint.
                    Again, Madame,
I implore you to reveal his name."


"You must not press me further," she replied
"I have the strength to keep as secret that
Which I believe should not be told."


Each ringing word was heard
By M. de Nemours, so close to them
And hidden in the small pavilion room,
Which smelt of boards, geranium and dust.
And what Mme de Clèves had said had made
Him no less jealous than M. de Clèves.
For, desperately in love with her, he thought

All men must equally be so, and doubt
Sprang like a fire across a forest floor.

He thought how slight now seemed the evidence
On which he based his hopes that it was he
Whom she now loved. Why had M. de Clèves
Not pressed her to divulge that secret name?

M. de Clèves was still intent to find
A name with which to grapple with his foe.
His wife said,
                    "Be content that I have not
Revealed my feelings; nor has anyone
Offended me by word or deed.
But ask nothing more."

"Ah!  Madame," M. de Clèves cried loudly. "I
Cannot believe you!  I recall the day
Your portrait vanished. I see now
That portrait — which was mine and which I loved —
You offered as a present to this man."

The princess answered, "Is it possible
That you should find duplicity
In the confession I have freely made?
I beg you to believe me. I did not
Give anyone the portrait.
                    And I saw
It being taken but I could say nothing
Because I feared to do so would invite
Some declaration by him and such words
As no-one has yet dared to say."

"Forgive me, Madame," he said. "I am unjust.
Refuse to answer but allow me this:
Do not rebuke me if I ask again."

Just then, some servants entered with the news
That M. de Clèves was sought. A gentleman
Had come with messages brought from the King
To summon him to Paris.
                              M. de Clèves
Was obliged to leave and could say nothing more
To his wife than to request she follow him
To Paris and to assure her tenderly
Of his esteem and love.

Mme de Clèves was suddenly alone.
And when she contemplated what had passed
She was so horrified that nothing seemed
Quite real
            or, rather, she could not believe
That she had said the smallest part of these
Appalling, echoing words.

But surely, she assured herself
Amidst alarm, this was the only way
To protect herself from M. de Nemours.
                                          Alone,
She spent the night tormented by
Uncertainty, fear and confusion.
                                    Nonetheless
She felt a certain sweetness in surrendering
So great a token of fidelity
To her husband who deserved so much, and who
Regarded her with such esteem.

Meanwhile M. de Nemours had left
The outer room and passed unseen
Through flower beds into the forest.
Quite suddenly
He thought the matter of the stolen portrait
Told in his favour.
                              Mme de Clèves
Had made it clear he was the man she loved.

And yet the very fact of her confession
Seemed in a way to relegate him still
To a distant ante-room, far from her heart.
He felt a sudden gust of cold despair.

In short, he knew delirious happiness
And sombre loneliness.
                              Night caught him unawares
And it was only with some difficulty
That he found a path back to his sister's house.

His explanations were quite awkward (dawn
Looked on him less complicitly).
                              That afternoon
With the Vidame he travelled back to Paris.

M. de Nemours was so preoccupied
With love — like one who travels, carrying
At his side a secret store of gold —
                              that he,
Departing from his usual good judgement,
Was seriously indiscreet:

Once back in Paris he could not refrain
From talking volubly of love. He told

His own experience in general terms
Or in a way purporting to be that
Of someone else.

     He told
The Vidame de Chartres about Mme de Clèves
While neither naming her nor acknowledging
This passionate narrative was his.

       The Vidame
Was not deceived: this wonderment and warmth
Was clearly Nemours' own. He urged his friend
To say so. But Nemours drew tightly to his side
The treasure of his love

       regretting having said so much.


M. de Clèves had visited the King;
But mortal sorrow pierced his heart.
Never had husband been so violently
In love nor held his wife in such regard.
All she had said increased his mourning love,
But all his thoughts turned on his need to know
Who had succeeded in the capture of her heart.


M. de Nemours occurred to him at once,
As forming, with the Chevalier de Guise
And the Maréchal de Saint-André, the three
Most dazzling stars in that brilliant firmament.
He was not listening properly to the King
Who told him he was chosen to escort
Madame, the daughter of the King, to Spain.
The King further affirmed that he believed
No-one would grace the party with more honour
Than Mme de Clèves.

      This opportunity
Might seem to give M. de Clèves a way

For them to leave the court quite naturally.
But this was still too far away
For present remedy.
                              M. de Clèves
At once wrote to his wife commanding her
Return to Paris. When they met
They both were overwhelmed by sadness.


He spoke of what weighed heavily in their thought:
"Your conduct gives me not the least concern
And you are stronger and more virtuous
Than you have thought. But still I am distressed
At feelings someone else inspires in you."


Mme de Clèves said, "Just to speak of it
Must make me die of shame. I beg of you,
Allow me to see no-one. Do not let
Me speak again of something which proclaims
My great unworthiness of you."


M. de Clèves said, "You are right, Madame,
I abuse your trust and kindness cruelly.
But have compassion, since you have aroused
In me a fearful curiosity
Which I have found impossible to bear
And I cannot prevent myself
                              from wondering
Whom I must envy most —
The Maréchal de Saint-André,
The Duc de Nemours or the Chevalier de Guise."


"I shall not answer," said Mme de Clèves,
Blushing. "Nor shall I ever give you grounds
To draw conclusions. But if I suspect

You are observing me with that in mind
I will not know how to behave at court.
In God's name, let me, on the pretext of
Some illness, see no-one."

"But no, Madame. It would be soon revealed
As mere pretence, arousing further questioning;
And furthermore I wish to place my trust
Entirely in your strength and character."

M. de Clèves was not mistaken.
                                        For his trust
So strengthened her against M. de Nemours
That she displayed a new austerity
Which no constraint could have achieved. And so
She visited the Reine Dauphine, she shone
At court, but none of this soft radiance
Fell on the Duc de Nemours.

He had believed that he was loved by her,
But now her actions and her distant gaze
Persuaded him that nothing he had heard
In that fragrant room was other than a dream.

One thing still gave him hope. He saw
The air of sadness which she could not hide.

One evening, when M. and Mme de Clèves
Were in the Queen's apartments, someone spoke
Of rumours that the King
Would soon appoint another nobleman
To accompany them to Spain. The choice
Was said to be the Chevalier de Guise
Or else the Maréchal de Saint-André.

M. de Clèves observed his wife. She gave
No least sign at the mention of these names;
He went into the King's room and returned
And said to her that he had heard
The nobleman who would accompany them
To Spain, was M. de Nemours.

Mme de Clèves was visibly disturbed.

Attempting to disguise her unrest, she said,
"This is a disagreeable choice for you;
He will share all the honours. Should you not
Try to have someone else?"

"Madame," he said, "it is not fear
Of sharing glory which affects you so. You are
Disturbed for other reasons. Have no fear.
What I said to you is not the truth.
I invented it in order to confirm
What I already know."
                          Upon these words,
He went out thinking he should not increase
His wife's extreme confusion. As he left,

M. de Nemours approached, and saw at once
Some cloud reflected in her face.
                          He spoke,
She looked at him not hearing what he said,
And, fearing that her husband might return,
She cried,
          "In God's name, leave me in peace!"

"Alas, Madame," he said, "I do little more
Than leave you in peace. What grounds have you for complaint?
I dare not speak, I dare not look, I tremble when
I come near you. What have I done
To deserve those words?"

Mme de Clèves regretted that she had
Allowed M. de Nemours this chance to speak
So openly, and left without reply.
She returned home, much agitated.
                                        M. de Clèves observed
How heightened her embarrassment now was,
And followed her into a private room.
"Do not avoid me, Madame," he said. "I shall
Say nothing to distress you. And I beg
You to forgive me for surprising you.
My punishment is my discovery
That Nemours was the one I feared above all others.
And yet I believe I love you with more tenderness,
More passion and more violence than the man
Your heart prefers."
                            At this, M. de Clèves
Burst into tears, tears soon mixed with his wife's,
As she embraced him with such tenderness
And sorrow that they did not speak again.

The preparations for the wedding of Madame
Were well advanced. The Duc d'Albe
Arrived and was received with ceremony.
The court was filled with billowing silks.
The King despatched to meet him several noblemen:
The Prince de Condé, the Cardinal de Lorraine,
The Cardinal de Guise, the Ducs de Lorraine, d'Aumale,
De Bouillon, de Guise and de Nemours.

The King himself stood waiting at the Louvre gate
With several hundred gentlemen.
And when d'Albe arrived, the King walked with him
To the apartments of Madame
To whom was brought a gift of great magnificence.

Assemblies at the Louvre were arranged
To show the Duc d'Albe the galaxies
Of beauties from the Paris court.
Reluctantly Mme de Clèves was present,
Relieved to find M. de Nemours had gone
To accompany M. de Savoie.

The Vidame de Chartres
                          could not put aside
His curiosity about his friend,
M. de Nemours, whose tale most certainly
Had seemed of no-one but himself.
                          The Vidame
Had watched Nemours with interest, but the court's
Planned nuptials and the arrival there of both
The Duc d'Albe and M. de Savoie
Had thrown a floral veil of high romance
Over the signs which otherwise
Might tell the truth about M. de Nemours.

The fragrance of orange blossom filled the air
Sustaining curiosity in the Vidame;
The natural impulse to confide
In one's most recent love made him repeat
To Mme de Martigues that most intriguing tale
Of one who freely told her husband of
Her passion for another man.
And furthermore he thought Nemours had been

The object of this lady's passion.

                                      The Vidame
Urged Mme de Martigues to watch Nemours
To help him ascertain the truth.
Mme de Martigues most readily agreed.


Some days before the wedding, Mme de Clèves
Was late attending court so that she met
The gentleman the Reine Dauphine had sent
To fetch her. When she reached the court
Mme la Dauphine was waiting on her bed
To tell her something of great urgency.


Mme de Clèves knelt by her bed. By chance
Her face was shadowed.

                            You know," said the Reine Dauphine,
"How curious we have been about the change
In M. de Nemours. I think I know the truth.
The man is desperately in love

                                and much loved in return
By one of this court's greatest beauties."


Mme de Clèves perhaps from modesty,
But certainly because she wished to think
That no-one knew the secrets of her heart,
Could not apply such rumours to herself.
She found herself, therefore, once more disturbed.


She said:
                "Is this surprising?  M. de Nemours
Is handsome and admired."


"Indeed, so. That is not the surprising part."
Mme la Dauphine continued eagerly.

"It is this: the woman who now loves Nemours
Has never given him the slightest sign;
Instead, for fear of giving in to her passion,
She has confessed her feelings to her husband,
Begging him to take her from the court.
And, what is more, the source of all of this
Is M. de Nemours himself."

                    Mme de Clèves
Knelt by the bed, her face against its rough,
Embroidered silk, fire burning in her face.
She could not speak.

                The Reine Dauphine,
So full of these disclosures, did not see
Mme de Clèves much discomposed; who, then
Recovering, said, "This seems hardly plausible;
Madame, I'm curious. Who has told you this?"

"Why, from Mme de Martigues who heard it from
The Vidame de Chartres who in turn
Learnt of it from the Duc de Nemours himself."

A shadow passed across the counterpane,
Succeeded by the Reine Dauphine's surprised,
Delighted cry.
                Mme de Clèves looked up.
The light was dazzling.
                        Shadows stepped aside.
She saw M. de Nemours.
                        The Reine Dauphine
Cried, "Here he is!  Now we can ask him for
The truth!"
                Mme de Clèves in haste moved close

And whispered to the Reine Dauphine that she,
At all costs, must not speak to him
About this, lest this breach of confidence
By the Vidame divide them.

                       Mme la Dauphine
Laughed as she spoke. "M. de Nemours,
You dress with even greater elegance."
And, with a corresponding charm, he said,
"I think I may without temerity
Conclude that you were speaking of me
And were about to ask me something which
Mme de Clèves seeks to prevent."

Mme la Dauphine said, "That is true. But I
Will not indulge her as I usually do.
And so I ask you this: are you the man
Who is in love with, and is loved, by one
Who hides her passion, yet confesses it
To her husband?"
                  Mme de Clèves'
Confusion and embarrassment were such
That, had death come to rescue her, she would
Have welcomed it with joy.
But M. de Nemours
Was even more unsettled by her words.
He saw at once
                 that he had placed Mme de Clèves
In such a grave predicament that she
Had every reason to detest him now.

Mme la Dauphine saw his embarrassment
And smiled and said in triumph, "Look at him
And judge if he is not the man we seek."
M. de Nemours was desperately aware

That he must find a way out of these woods,
And at a stroke regained his wits and said:

"I do confess, Madame, that it would be
Most difficult to be more startled than I am,
That the Vidame de Chartres has betrayed my trust
By telling you the story of my friend —
Which I had told him in the strictest confidence.
But I shall exact revenge."
He smiled and spoke so calmly that he saw
Mme la Dauphine's suspicions set at rest.
"For he has told me certain things himself
Which I may one day use. But why,
Madame, you see in me that lucky man
Whose story I related to the Vidame
I cannot think. I may, perhaps,
Be thought to be a man in love but not,
I fear, a love requited."

With this last sentiment M. de Nemours
Hoped to distract his questioner with thoughts
Of his behaviour towards her in the past.

"I was distressed," he said, "for my friend's sake
And by the thought of his reproach. And yet
He told me only part of his heart's secrets
And never named the person whom he loves."
He looked at her with sadness. "I believe
No-one is more deserving of our pity."

"But surely," said the Reine Dauphine, "his love
Is a requited love. Is pity quite
Appropriate?"
                    "Do you believe, Madame,

A woman who was truly passionate
Could calmly tell her husband of her fears?
She is, as yet, quite ignorant of love.
My friend has little hope, I fear. And yet
Unhappy as he is, he thinks himself
Most fortunate to have at least made her
Afraid to fall in love with him, and so
Would not change places with any other man."

Mme la Dauphine remarked that, after all,
It seemed the story may be just a fiction
As Mme de Clèves had thought.

"That is indeed my view," said Mme de Clèves,
Who had been silent.
"But even were it possible these things occurred,
How could it ever have been widely known?
A woman capable of such extraordinary strength
Would hardly be so weak as, afterwards,
To speak of it. Nor would her husband break
So dangerous a confidence — unless
He was unworthy of her trust."
                                M. de Nemours
Encouraged such suspicions. "Jealousy,"
He said, "can make a husband indiscreet."

Mme de Clèves felt at the boundaries
Of strength and courage.
The arrival of Mme de Valentinois,
With news that the King would soon arrive, gave her
Relief and an excuse to leave.
                        The Reine Dauphine
Went to her private room to dress.
Mme de Clèves

Was following her when M. de Nemours
Said urgently,
              "Madame, I would give my life
To speak to you, but, of the many things
Which I might say I beg you to believe
That anything I said to Mme la Dauphine
Which seemed to apply to her was said
For reasons that have nothing to do with her."

Mme de Clèves seemed to hear none of this;
She left him without speaking. As she turned
To follow through the crowd to where the King
Moved with his courtiers,
                          she caught her dress
And fell. This gave her an excuse
To escape a place which emptied her of strength
And be escorted home.

M. de Clèves came to the Louvre,
                          and there,
He was surprised to find his wife absent.

He learnt about her accident, and at once
Went home to her. He found her in her bed
And soon discovered that her injury
Was slight.
              Yet there was something more.

She seemed wrapped in a cloak of sadness.
"Something is wrong, Madame," he said.
"A pain greater than that caused by your fall
Afflicts you."

"I could not be more troubled," she replied.
"You have misused the extraordinary —
Or, rather, foolish — trust I placed in you.
Did I dream that you would tell the world?
Were you so curious to obtain a name
That you abused my confidence
In the attempt to discover it?
                                                Someone
Has just repeated to me all that I
Told you and you alone,
Not knowing I was that unfortunate
And trusting wife."

"Madame, you cannot possibly believe
That I would speak of it. You must have heard
A story of some other woman."

"No, no, Monsieur," she cried. "There could not be
Another story like mine in the world,
No other woman capable of such a thing.
The Reine Dauphine told me;
She heard it from the Vidame de Chartres
Who had it from M. de Nemours."

"M. de Nemours!" exclaimed M. de Clèves
With wild despair. "You say M. de Nemours
Knows that you love him and, what's more,
Knows that you have told me?"

"You seem to single out M. de Nemours
Repeatedly.
                    But I have said
I will not comment on your list of names.
M. de Nemours had heard it from a friend

Who must be equally a friend of yours
And whom you trusted with my confidence."

"Would any man in my position tell
The very fact which he would hide from himself?
Rather I think it you, Madame,
Who, finding such a secret insupportable
Sought out the confidante who has in turn
Betrayed your secret."

Mme de Clèves cried out,
                            "Would you destroy me utterly?
Can you be harsh enough to find in me
The fault you have yourself committed?
Could you believe me capable of such a thing?"

A long, diaphanous brocade
Of mutual bewilderment entwined itself
About them;
                    they fell silent.
                            Far worse
Than this confusion was the certainty
That soon their secret would be widely known.

At first, almost united by
Their puzzlement,
                        as dusk approached, they lapsed
Into the same reproaches. Then the sash
Which bound them in its coils, began
To disentwine itself.
                            Their hearts and minds
Were led into a more estranging grief
Than they had ever known.

The night was starless; dawn seemed long delayed.
M. de Clèves slept fitfully. He thought
About the fact that he no longer knew
What he should think about Mme de Clèves.
He did not know
How he desired her to behave, nor how
He should behave himself.

At last, after a period
Of agitation and uncertainty,
In which he saw dark chasms on every side,

He thought that because they soon must leave for Spain,
They must meanwhile insist these revelations
Were mere fiction.
                  Most importantly,
Mme de Clèves should still appear at court.

When morning came at last with wreathing mists,
M. de Clèves went to his wife,
Exhorting her to share this policy;
The Duc de Nemours must think the story false,
She must convince him by indifference.

Mme de Clèves was left alone.
She walked through shadows in the curtained room.
Outside the grove was peopled still in mist
Like figures mingling at the court.
                       She felt
Such anger with M. de Nemours, it seemed
Indifference would be easy to sustain.

And she would be obliged to be at court
And show a public face calmly composed,

Especially for the wedding ceremonies,
Since, of the several princesses,
She had been chosen to support the train
Of the Reine Dauphine.
                              And so she spent the day
Alone, in her rooms, preparing to suppress
Her feelings.
                    Most difficult of these
Was knowing she could not exonerate
M. de Nemours. She could not doubt
That he had told the story to the Vidame;
He had confessed as much. Nor could she doubt
He knew the story was of her.
                                        Where was
The discretion which she had admired in him?


"He was discreet while ever he could not
Have hope, but at the prospect of success,
He had to speak of it.
                            And I was wrong
To think that any man was capable
Of hiding that which flattered self-esteem.
And yet it is for this man, whom I thought
So different from other men, that I
Became like other women,
                                    and so lost
The affection of the husband in whose love
I ought to have been happy.


I shall be soon condemned
As one who has surrendered to a wild
And violent passion. Yet it was
To avoid this very thing I spoke the truth."

These bitter thoughts were followed by a flood of tears.

M. de Nemours himself was hardly less
Disturbed. His indiscretion and the thoughts
Of Mme de Clèves, her face so pale and troubled,
Appalled him now.
                    "What should I say to her?
Through my own negligence I gave to her
A more effective shield with which to arm
Herself against me than she might have found
In all her struggles otherwise,
                                    a defence
She may have sought in vain.

By indiscretion I have forfeited
The hope of being loved by her
Who is more worthy of esteem than any other.
Yet worse than this
Is the certainty that I have harmed her too."

Tormented by this irreversible,
Large-looming fact, M. de Nemours
Traversed and retraversed the same dark thoughts.
Desire to speak to Mme de Clèves returned
Incessantly.
                But he determined that
Most politic would be to show respect
By a sorrowing silence, even to appear
Reluctant to intrude upon her presence,
And to await whatever favour time
And chance might bring.

The preparations for the weddings, which
Were soon to take place on the following day

Preoccupied the court.
                              Mme de Clèves
And M. de Nemours had little difficulty
In hiding their unhappiness.

The betrothals of Madame, the daughter of the King
And Marguerite, his sister, dawned to glistening air.
The Louvre billowed like a ship in sail;
And that magnificence of form and colour spread
To ball and banquet, after which
The parties went to spend the festive night
At the Bishop's Palace, as was customary.
And in the morning's brilliance the Duc d'Albe
In coat of cloth of gold, bejewelled, crossed
By bands of fiery red and black and yellow,
With all the Spanish entourage set out
From the Hôtel de Villeroy to the Bishop's Palace.
The Duc de Savoie with his attendants,
Was feted by the King and Queen, the Reine Dauphine,
Mme de Lorraine, the Queen of Navarre, their trains
Held out by princesses. The ball resumed,
Still interspersed with ballets, banquets and tableaux.

Throughout the ceremonies, unhappy as she was,
Mme de Clèves shone out like sun on snow
And seemed to all
                              incomparably beautiful.
The Duc de Nemours particularly observed
This radiance
                    but dared not speak to her,
Despite the opportunities of the crowds.
And such was his expression of respect
And gravity,
                              Mme de Clèves

No longer found him quite as culpable;
And in the following days her heart once more
Restored him to its former place.

The tournament was soon to crown these joys.
The ladies moved into the galleries,
Like stars which have the power to gaze and applaud
While dazzling everyone who sees them. Next,
The four appointed champions joined the lists
With many horses and attendants robed
In livery. It was
The finest vision ever seen in France.

The King wore white and black as always, for
Mme de Valentinois; M. de Guise
Appeared in white and rose-pink, faithful to
A former love now lost; M. de Ferrare,
And all his retinue, yellow and red. M. de Nemours
Wore black and yellow; no-one understood
This choice except Mme de Clèves, who knew
That he had overheard her say
That yellow was a colour which she loved
But could not wear because she was so fair.
And thus without the slightest risk
Of indiscretion, he could blazon forth her favour.

The skill displayed by those four champions was
Incomparable. Although the King was said
To be the finest horseman in the land
It was impossible to judge between them.
M. de Nemours had elegance and grace;
Each time that he successfully appeared
Mme de Clèves could scarce conceal her joy.

As dusk approached and everyone prepared
To leave,
            the King announced that he would like
To break one further lance.
He sent a message ordering
The Comte de Montgomery to join him in the lists.
This splendid horseman begged him not to joust;
The King insisted that they meet once more
Now, in the dusk. The Queen sent messengers
Asking the King not to remount. He said,
That he would ride once more for love of her
And passed into the field.
                          They ran their course.
The lances broke.
                          And then a splinter from
Montgomery's lance entered and lodged in
The King's eye. He fell at once. The squires
Ran to assist him.

The King was carried to his bed.
The surgeons found his wound to be most grave.

For several days before his final breath
The King displayed great fortitude. The court
Became a crowded and disordered hive.
The prophecy was recalled in solemn tones
Amongst the concourse in the ante-room;
The Queen stayed almost constantly at his side.

Mme de Clèves knew well that she could not
Avoid the court, and therefore that she must
See M. de Nemours. She feared
Her resolution must dissolve like snow
In rain. And as she feigned once more

An illness which in all the confusion of the court
No-one questioned,
                    M. de Clèves
Brought news, each day more sombre, of the King.
His manner to her seemed as courteous,
And yet a little colder than before.
They spoke only of the King.


M. de Nemours was puzzled and distressed
At each day's absence of Mme de Clèves.


In just ten days, between the tournament
And the funeral of the King,
                              forces of change
Had quite transformed the swarming hive at court:
The Queen (who now became the Queen Mother)
Shook off some troublesome and clinging courtiers;
Diane de Poitiers was driven from the court;
The new Queen, formerly the Reine Dauphine,
Was grudgingly acceded to; the Duc de Guise
Attained new power, while others were consigned
To distant shores on diplomatic pretexts.


A casualty of the new order was
The journey of M. de Clèves to Spain
And, while he felt ambitions thwarted there,
His chief regret was that his wife would lose
The opportunity to leave the court.


A few days later, when it was decreed
The coronation should take place at Reims
And all the court attend,
                          Mme de Clèves,
Persisting with her illness, asked that she

Should travel rather to Coulommiers;
The fresh air there, she said, would aid her health.
Her husband said that he had no desire
To know if this were genuine or not,
But willingly consented — since he had
Already felt alarm that she should be
Exposed in Reims to the gaze of one she loved.


M. de Nemours soon learned
Mme de Clèves
Was not to accompany the court to Reims.
He felt he could not leave without
An attempt to see her.
                              So, on the final night,
At as late an hour as decorum would allow,
He called on her, and in the courtyard met
Mme de Nevers and Mme de Martigues
Who said she was alone.
                              He went up in a state
Of agitation and confusion which
Could only be compared to that
Of Mme de Clèves when he was announced.
                                                  She feared
That he might speak to her too passionately
And she reply too favourably.
                              She feared
To tell and not to tell M. de Clèves
Of such a visit, and impulsively
She drew back from the thing
                              that she desired
Most in the world,
                 to see and speak
With M. de Nemours.

She sent a servant to M. de Nemours
To tell him that she had been taken ill
And could not accept the honour of his visit.
With harsh regret Nemours retraced his steps.
He had not spoken to Mme de Clèves
Since that most painful conversation with
The Reine Dauphine.

                He thought continually
Of this and of its cause — his vanity,
The error of confiding in the Vidame.
Tomorrow he must leave for Reims
With none of this divisiveness resolved,
And no way to address Mme de Clèves.


As soon as he had gone,
The reasons for dismissing him,
Which had seemed so persuasive, disappeared.
Had it been possible, Mme de Clèves
Believed she should have sent
The servant to recall M. de Nemours.


M. de Clèves, most vulnerable of men,
Was in the Queen's apartments when
Mme de Nevers and Mme de Martigues returned.
The Queen asked them where they had been, and who
Had been in that company.

                He heard them name
His wife, his house, then heard them say
That when they left, "only M. de Nemours
Was there." These words, which seemed so innocent,
Were to M. de Clèves a flame.

                And jealousy
Blazed freshly, and he left at once for home,
Not even knowing what he hoped to find.

Arriving home he felt anxious relief
To find Nemours had gone. He went at once
To join his wife, and for a while conversed
On some indifferent matters. Then he asked
What she had done and whom she had seen. She told him.
She did not mention M. de Nemours. He asked
Had she seen no-one else? She said with truth
That she had not.
              "And what about
M. de Nemours? Or had you forgotten him?"
"No," she replied. "I did not see him; nor
Have I forgotten him. He came,
He asked for me, but I felt ill and so
Sent someone down to him to make my excuses."

"And so you felt ill only for his sake?
As you saw others, why make this excuse
For him? Why is he not the same for you
As other men? Why are you so afraid
And let him see you are afraid, and thus
Confer such power upon him? Would you dare
Refuse him if you did not know that he
Distinguishes between your passionate fear
And mere discourtesy?"

"However much you may suspect
M. de Nemours, I never would have thought
You would reproach me for not seeing him."

"I do reproach you, Madame," he said.
"If he has, as you claimed, said nothing to you,
Then why not see him?
              But it is clear, Madame,
That he has spoken to you. Silent looks

Could not make such an impression on you. You
Could not confess the whole truth and you hid
The greater part of it.
                              I am
Unhappier than I thought. You are my wife,
I love you as a mistress. Yet I am forced
To recognise that you love another
Who sees you every day and has no doubts
That he is loved."


"Perhaps," Mme de Clèves sadly replied,
"You were mistaken to approve
A gesture as extraordinary as mine,
And I perhaps as wrong
To think that you would still be fair to me."


"Indeed," rejoined M. de Clèves, "we were
Both much mistaken. What you hoped of me
Was as impossible
As all that I hoped for from you. I thought —
Quite foolishly — that you might overcome
Your passion for him.
                              You in turn supposed
That I was capable
Of being rational. Had you forgotten then
I was your husband and I loved you desperately?
For either reason any man might find himself
In some extremities. What then if both applied?


I am a prey to violent feeling which
I cannot master, I adore
Then hate you, I admire then feel ashamed
At admiration, I despise myself
Then find that it is you

To whom such feelings turn. There is, in short
Neither tranquillity nor reason in me now.

I cannot think how I have lived since that
Still unreceding afternoon at Coulommiers
Or since the day the Reine Dauphine revealed
That others knew your story.
                                        Nor can I understand
By what means it has been divulged.
I ask no more of you
But to remember you have made of me
The unhappiest of men."

They said no more. M. de Clèves, without
Seeing Mme de Clèves again,
Set out the following day for Reims,
                                        but wrote
A letter full of sorrow, courtesy
And kindness.
                        And Mme de Clèves' reply
Was touching, gentle and abounded in
Assurances both in regard to past
And future, sentiments so genuine
The letter brought M. de Clèves
Some measure of tranquillity.

Her husband's courtesy would for a time
Suffuse with cloud the image of
M. de Nemours.
                        But soon that image grew
In light and power once more and filled her mind.

For some days after his departure for Reims,
She thought she had not missed him; then at once

She felt it cruelly.
                    She went to Coulommiers,
Unsure if she might find in woods and fields
Some trace or semblance of her loneliness.

She took with her a set of paintings, prized
Because they celebrated notable
Achievements in the late King's reign.
                                    In one,
Amongst the heroes of the siege of Metz,

M. de Nemours was pictured. This, perhaps,
Had influenced her choice.

Mme de Martigues, who had not gone to Reims,
Spent several days with her at Coulommiers.
Their roles as favourites of the new Queen
Had never led to rivalry; they were friends
But did not share their deepest secrets. Thus
Mme de Clèves knew of her friend, that she
Loved the Vidame; that friend however had
No knowledge of the turbulence of heart
Of Mme de Clèves.

Her guest found Mme de Clèves devoted to
The pursuit of solitude. She spent the days
Alone amongst the garden flowers and trees.
Sometimes she visited the pavilion
Not knowing it was here M. de Nemours
Had overheard her passionate secret.

Mme de Martigues was charmed by Coulommiers
And in particular the avenue
And, at its turning under ancient trees,

The pavilion.
                    There the two spent many hours
In affectionate conversation, savouring
The pleasures of true confidence which yet
Withheld one luminous secret.

Mme de Martigues was only drawn away
From these delightful days at Coulommiers
By learning that the court had now left Reims
And (with the Vidame de Chartres) were resident
At the château just completed at Chambord.
The Queen was pleased to see Mme de Martigues;
She asked for news of Mme de Clèves
And heard a full account
Of the grave beauty of Coulommiers.
Mme de Martigues described the avenues,
The pavilion bordering the woods, and stressed
The pleasures taken by Mme de Clèves
In walking there at night.
                    M. de Clèves
And M. de Nemours were present.
                            Both could see
The pavilion set amongst the trees.

M. de Clèves observed M. de Nemours
In conversation with Mme de Martigues.

He had no doubts
                    of what was in his rival's mind.

M. de Nemours next day asked leave of the King
To go to Paris.
                    M. de Clèves, afraid
His own departure might alert

M. de Nemours,
     employed a trusted gentleman
And ordered him to follow M. de Nemours,
Observe him closely and report whether
At night he entered the garden.

This gentleman watched M. de Nemours
Who did not pause until he reached a village
Not far from Coulommiers. The gentleman
Thought that Nemours would stay there until dusk,
And went ahead to wait.
     As soon as night
Had fallen, he heard someone on the path
And in the gloom could recognise Nemours.

The stout, high fences were an obstacle
And there were others ranged beyond the first,
Which made his entry difficult.

The Duc de Nemours entered the garden.
He saw bright lamps in many windows.
He approached the pavilion in such trepidation
It seemed he heard his heartbeat in the trees.
The windows stood wide open.
     She was alone,
And unimaginably beautiful in the light.
The night was hot.
     She wore, on her head
And shoulders, nothing but her loosened hair.

She was reclining on a day-bed, at her side
A table holding several baskets, filled
With coloured ribbons.
     She picked out some of these.

Nemours could see they were the very colours
He had carried at the tournament.

He saw that she was tying these in bows
On a quite unusual malacca cane
Which had undoubtedly been his, and which
He then had given to his sister.
                                    It seemed
Mme de Clèves knew that it had been his.
How had she taken it?
                              This idle task
She finished with such grace it seemed to him
All of her heart was written on her face.

And now she took a lighted candlestick
And went to a large table over which
Was hung the painting of the siege of Metz.
She sat before it gazing with a rapt
And concentrated attention.

To stand in darkness and admire in light
The woman he adored,
                              to see her now
Clearly absorbed with thoughts of him
                                                and see revealed
The passion she had hidden from his gaze —
What lover has known such supreme delight?

Beside himself,
                    he remained transfixed,
Uncertain whether to approach and speak to her.
She was so near,
                    and yet he thought it wise
To wait until she came into the garden,

For then her servants should not hear her voice.

And yet she did not leave this room,
                              but gazed,
Still, at the painting. Now he thought perhaps
He should go in,
                    but feared alarming her
And seeing that soft candle bloom of thought
Turn into anger or severity.

He felt that this was madness — to attempt
To speak, to startle her with love
Which he had never spoken of before,
To hope that she might listen in this dark,
Crowded with dangers.
                        Better
To see her silently in candlelight
Afloat against the dark.
                        And suddenly
His rapture faltered. Its poor candle flame
Guttered. A cold gust of fear
Became a roaring in the dark trees,
And several times
                    he was about to turn
And leave this window into which the world
Had concentrated all its light.
                        Instead,
Desiring still to speak to her
He moved impulsively.
                        He stumbled, or a scarf
Caught in the open window with a noise;
Mme de Clèves turned. Perhaps because
Her mind already framed his image, or,
Perhaps because the light flowed out

Sufficiently to reach his face,
                                        she thought
She saw him in the darkness.
                                        Then she rose
And left the room at once.

She was disturbed and shaken and unwell.

Reflecting further, it seemed that, possibly,
She had been quite mistaken and had thought,
Because her mind had dwelt so long on it,
The darkness must contain his face.

She knew that he was with the court at Chambord.
His presence here should seem unlikely.
                                        Yet
The impulse to return, and venture out
Into the garden troubled her
                                        until
She was surprised to see the lightening sky.

M. de Nemours lingered in the warm,
Expectant air of lavender and musk;
But when the servants closed the doors he knew
That he would not be fortunate again.
He went back through the forest to his horse;
The gentleman discreetly followed him.

M. de Nemours returned the following night.
He spent the intervening day
Divided between joy at seeing her
Preoccupied with thoughts of him,
And deep dismay at her apparent fear
Of meeting him.

He walked a little way
Beneath the willows' combed and shimmering hair
Beside a stream. He sought a solitary bank
So as to indulge the sweetly bitter tears
Of love, its alternating sun and cloud.

He spoke aloud, he pressed the willow wands
Against his face, he listened to the stream;
He said,
        "She loves me, yet is more severe
Than if she hated me. Were she indifferent,
I could attempt to please her, and she might
Grow kind; but she is not indifferent.
So she protects herself with equal zeal
From me and from herself."

Between the willow branches in full leaf
He came upon a grotto where the stream
Was blocked and eddied in a curtained pool.
He cried, "Princess! If only once you might
Look out at me as you were looking at
My portrait!"

That night he went to Coulommiers again,
Again tethering his horse below an oak
And walking through the woods. The pavilion
Was dark, the doors were closed. Mme de Clèves,
Suspecting that she had not been deceived
In seeing him, and that he might return,
Had kept within her rooms.
                     M. de Nemours
Remained with fading hopes until the moon,
A waning sliver, rose through woods and passed
Above the sombre trees.

                        Faint signs of dawn
And fears of being seen forced him to leave.

But now it seemed impossible
To go back to the shimmering of the court
Without seeing Mme de Clèves once more.

He went to see Mme de Mercoeur, who was
At this time in her house near Coulommiers.
Surprised and pleased to see her brother, she
Was easily prompted to suggest a visit
To Mme de Clèves.

When they arrived, she was in the avenue
Beside the flower maze. She was dismayed
To see M. de Nemours.
                        She knew at once
That she had seen him several nights before
Drawn like a moth at her window in the dark,
And now she felt annoyed by this imprudence.

He showed himself so very curious
To see the small pavilion in the woods,
Mme de Mercoeur exclaimed that from all he said
He must have been there several times.
                                "And yet,"
Said Mme de Clèves, "I do not think M. de Nemours
Has been inside it, it was only built
A little while ago." "It is not long,
In fact, since I was there," said M. de Nemours.
"Perhaps I should be flattered that you have
Forgotten that you saw me there."
                        Mme de Mercoeur
Was looking at the lilies in their beds

And did not notice what was being said.
Mme de Clèves contrived, by showing them
Details and points of interest, to prevent
Mme de Mercoeur discovering in the pavilion
Her brother's picture. Time passed steadily
And, for M. de Nemours, frustratingly;
He had hoped by some pretext to remain
After his sister left, but that time came
And Mme de Clèves, to prevent it, ordered her carriage
And accompanied them to the borders of the forest.


The gentleman returned to M. de Clèves,
Who waited with the rising certainty
That what he was to hear might well confirm
His life in ruin.
That gentleman said,
                  "I have no certainties;
M. de Nemours spent two successive nights
Within the forest, near the gardens, then
The following day again at Coulommiers
With Mme de Mercoeur."
                  "That is enough"
Cried M. de Clèves, "I need hear nothing more."


The gentleman withdrew, alarmed to see
The violence of despair, scarcely suppressed,
In M. de Clèves,
           who could not resist
The crushing sorrow and the stifling pain
Which must afflict a man of passionate heart
Who in a single moment finds confirmed
His mistress's infidelity and the shame
Of a trusted wife's deceit.
              That very night

M. de Clèves succumbed to fever, so
Overwhelming that his life appeared in danger.

Mme de Clèves was summoned. When she arrived,
She found an inexplicable,
Disturbing coldness in his manner to her
Which she could only think a consequence
Of his grave fever.

When she arrived at Blois to which the court
Had moved and where M. de Clèves now lay,
M. de Nemours could not help feeling joy
At the mere fact of her presence. But he found
She did not leave her husband's room, and was
Entirely given to concern for him.
The thought tormented him that this distress
Might reawaken her affections for
Her husband and cast out her love for him;
He even found himself considering
The change in his fortune which the death
Of M. de Clèves might bestow on him.

Meanwhile M. de Clèves
Was almost given up as lost.
The doctors could do nothing, and Mme de Clèves
Remained alone with him.
                           After a troubled night
He seemed distraught. She knelt by him, her face
Covered in tears.
                  "You shed many tears, Madame,
For a death which you yourself have caused, and which
Cannot be as distressing to you as you pretend.
I am no longer able to reproach you — "
He spoke so faintly she was obliged to bring

Her shining face near him to hear these words:
"But I am dying of the cruel blow
You struck me. Why did you reveal
Your passion for M. de Nemours if you
Could not resist it? Why did you not leave
Me in that state of blind happiness
Which many husbands share?"
       Mme de Clèves
Was lost in tears and did not hear at first
Or did not understand the flow of words,
Until she heard him say:
"…He is a man who makes a show of love
But thinks of nothing but seducing you.
Yet with this man, this M. de Nemours,
You spent two nights at Coulommiers."

She did not understand. She was amazed
At such a thought.
     "But how could such a thing
Be in your mind, unless the fever takes
You further from yourself? I never have
Passed any night nor even moments with
M. de Nemours. He has not spoken privately
To me. I swear upon my honour."
Interrupting her, M. de Clèves
Said, "Say no more. Hypocrisy
Or a complete confession — both would be
As painful to me."
      At first Mme de Clèves,
Speechless with tears and misery,
          could not reply.
At last she said, "If this concerned no-one but me
I could bear these reproaches. But it is your life
Which sways in these capricious winds.

                              Listen to me
For your own dear sake:  it is impossible
That with the truth you shall not be convinced
Of my innocence."


"I would that it were so," he cried. "But what
Is there to say?  Was not M. de Nemours
At Coulommiers with his sister?  Did he not
Spend two nights with you in the forest garden?"


Mme de Clèves saw suddenly
                              as if in noon's harsh light
The winding avenue down which M. de Clèves
Was led, the false and frightening vista —
                                             "No!"
She cried, "No!  I am not this woman who
Torments you. She does not exist.
If you will not believe me then, at least,
Believe your servants. Ask them, they will tell
That I remained indoors because I feared
The presence of M. de Nemours."


And then she told him earnestly
Of being, on that first night, in the room
Which looked out on the garden; the night was hot,
She heard a slight sound at the window. Then,
Like some moth drawn towards the light, it seemed
A face was floating on the dark night air,
Which for a moment seemed to be M. de Nemours.


She told him how at once she left the room
And on the next night, fearing his return,
Had not gone to the garden room. She spoke
With such conviction and such clarity

The truth rose to the surface like a foam
Spread glistening down the breaking wave
Of his despair.
                M. de Clèves almost
Again believed her innocent.

"I do not any longer know," he said,
"If anything is as believable
As I would wish. Your explanation comes
Too late, but it allows me some relief
To think you worthy of the esteem in which
I held you. Grant this consolation too,
That you will remember me with fondness
As one you might have loved as you love him
Had it been possible to will it so."

Faintness robbed him of speech. Mme de Clèves
Summoned the doctors who pronounced him close
To death; he lingered for a few more days.

Mme de Clèves was overtaken by such grief
That for a time she lost the power of thought
And in a state approaching vacancy
Was taken by the new Queen to a convent
Where, without remembering it, she rested.
When she was brought back to Paris,
                             still
She did not understand her state of mind.
But then she knew the husband she had lost
And saw that she herself had caused his death
And caused it by her passion for another man —
Then she was overcome
By horror, both at herself and M. de Nemours.

At first M. de Nemours dared only pay
To Mme de Clèves those decorous respects
Which mourning seemed to sanction. Then he learned
This grey decorum would assert itself
For longer than he had hoped:

                          an equerry
Informed him that it now was widely thought
The death of M. de Clèves was caused, in fact,
By his, Nemour's, night visits to Coulommiers.
He was surprised, but feared that, for a time,
Mme de Clèves might still resent his love.

He tried to stay away. Despite himself
He found himself outside her door to ask
For news of her.

                 It was relayed to him
That she saw no-one and her servants were
Forbidden to inform her who had called.

But  now he was so overwhelmingly
In love, he sought to find
The means to overcome these obstacles
Which seemed insurmountable.

Mme de Clèves increased in grief. She saw
Her husband who had died because of her
In every thought. She brooded endlessly
Resolving to do nothing in her life
Which he would not have wished, had he still lived.

She wondered how M. de Clèves had known
M. de Nemours had come to Coulommiers.
She did not think that gentleman would tell
Of such a failed excursion; nor did she care,

Convinced as she now was her passion had
Become an error of the past.
                              But even so,
She felt distressed at every thought of him
Who had caused her husband's death. This turbulence
Of feelings fell within the general
Pervasiveness of sorrow
                              and she thought
She had no other feelings.


After several months, this violence
Passed into melancholy.
                         Then Mme de Martigues
Began to visit her more frequently
And, hoping to distract her spoke once more
Of events at court.
                         She spoke of the Vidame,
M. de Guise — and his new power at court —
And then:
            "And as for poor M. de Nemours,
I cannot tell if public duties have
Dispelled all thoughts of love in him,
But he seems much withdrawn and seems to shun
The company of women."


Mme de Clèves was shaken by the name.
She blushed, and turned aside, and changed
The subject, and this flush went unobserved.


The following day, Mme de Clèves went out
To see a man whose house was close to hers
And who made articles in silk.
                              She thought
Her emptiness of heart might be employed

And filled by this pursuit.
He showed her samples and explained the art,
And then she saw a door which she supposed
Must lead to further stocks of silk. She asked,
And he replied this room was locked.
                                        He said
A gentleman had leased the room and came
Sometimes to sketch the houses, visible
From its window.
                        "He is a handsome gentleman.
He hardly looks as if he needs to earn
A living. Often when he comes he stands
And gazes from the window but, I think,
I've never seen him draw."
                                    Mme de Clèves
Remembered that Mme de Martigues had said
M. de Nemours was in Paris.
Mme de Clèves was curious about this man
Who came to a house so close to hers. She went
To the windows and looked out. She found her house
And all her garden were clearly visible.
Indeed, on her return, she went at once
And, looking from her window, easily saw
The window where the unknown stranger stood.

The thought, that this mysterious gentleman —
Who came to gaze and draw but did not draw —
Might even be M. de Nemours, disturbed her.
Her melancholy, almost tranquil mood
Gave way to agitation and unease.
And, finally, this restlessness
Led her to walk some distance to a grove
Where she could be alone.
                                    She saw no-one.

She walked, as if attempting to escape
From herself; she passed through woods and, where the path
Diverged into a maze of paths,
                              she paused:
A summer-house, open on all sides
Stood near some trees. And then she saw a man
Reclining on some benches, lost in thought.
She recognised M. de Nemours.
                              He seemed
So distant, in so fixed a reverie,
That when he rose and went towards the gates
To where his carriage waited silently
She felt that she was in another world
And, even had she had the will to speak
And let herself be noticed, she could not
Have reached him.

What turmoil this brief glimpse of him released!
How violently her passion had returned
In just the time she took to walk towards
The summer house, and sit where he had sat.
His image lingered like the effusive air
Of roses at Coulommiers at dusk;
His qualities pressed round her:  he had loved
With tact and patience, honouring the time
Of her bereavement; shunning the displays
Of court and choosing solitude, he watched
The garden where she cultivated grief,
But did not seek to speak to her. He was,
In short, the very model of restraint,
Consideration and respect;
And suddenly she saw that now there were
No obstacles, nothing now remained
Of their past circumstances but their passion.

These thoughts seemed strangely new.
It was as if
In her bereavement she had thought of nothing.
M. de Nemours was suddenly quite real.
He had not seen her and had walked towards
The furthest gates, and in that avenue
Had vanished in his coach.

                          And yet
This same M. de Nemours had caused the death
Of M. de Clèves, who, as he died, had said
He feared that she might marry him. This thought
Struck like a sword across the billowing silks
Of all these others.

                So she was convinced
That any thought of marrying M. de Nemours
Was scarcely less a crime than loving him
While her husband was alive,
And duty should impel her to avoid,
At all costs, seeing him.

                  She gave herself
To these reflections, fatal as they were
To all her hopes of happiness.
But this conviction failed to win her heart;
That night was one of the cruellest she had known.


Her waking impulse was to go at once
And see if there were anyone looking out
Across her garden at her house.

                  She went
Towards the window. She saw the man.

                        She stepped back
In such surprise M. de Nemours could guess
He had been recognised.

                  But still he was

No closer to discovering the means
Of speaking to her.

He had been reticent;
He had allowed her time for mourning, but
Now feared that this may well have been a time
For her to reason with her heart.

The Vidame was in Paris. M. de Nemours
Decided to confide in him. He spoke
Of his devotion in the strongest terms.
This news was greeted with delight;
The Vidame assured his friend that, ever since
The Princess had become a widow,

                               he had thought
She was the only woman worthy of him.

Her uncle suggested that the two should meet;
Nemours was cautious, for, in mourning still,
She might resent too obvious an approach.
They thought it best if the Vidame,

                           on some pretext,
Were to invite her, and M. de Nemours
Arrive as if by chance.

Mme de Clèves was startled when Nemours
Appeared. The Vidame spoke of various things,
And then excused himself, asking his niece
To entertain his friend till he returned.

At last alone and able to converse
They were for some time speechless.
They heard the silence of the hour-glass,
The silence of the glade in which the bees

Are heard within their hive.

M. de Nemours spoke:

"Will you forgive M. de Chartres, Madame,
For giving me the opportunity
To see you and converse with you (which you
Have always cruelly denied)?"

"I cannot do so," she replied, "for he
Forgets my reputation and the risk
To me were we to be seen."

"You need not fear, Madame," he said. "No-one
Knows I am here.
I entered by a private stair-case.

But, Madame,
I beg of you, listen, if not for my sake
Then for your own, to spare you the excess
To which I should be driven irresistibly
By a passion I can not control."

Mme de Clèves yielded a little.
She glanced at him, and in that glance he read
Faint signs of gentleness and gaiety
Like faded figures in an old romance.
She said,

"But what could you expect of happiness
Were I to give consent?
Our fate has not been joyful in the past.
Might you not find what you deserve elsewhere?"

"Elsewhere!" he cried. "What happiness could there be
But to be loved by you?
Although I have not spoken openly
You must have known and seen

My passion is as violent and true
As anyone will ever feel.

Has it not been put to the test again
And again, by your refusals?"
Mme de Clèves replied,
"It is true. Not only have I noticed it
But understood it as you would have wished."

"Then if you have, Madame, is it possible
That you were not affected by this knowledge?"

"My conduct must have pointed to as much
By all it sought to hide.
              And yet I wonder
What conclusions you had drawn."

"My great unhappiness prevented me
From making any vain assumption. Hope
Seemed always part of everything I thought
And I had cast hope out.
              This I can say:
I wished with all my heart
That you had not confessed to M. de Clèves
All you concealed from me."

Mme de Clèves said:
              "I could never understand
How you were able to discover
The secrets I confessed to M. de Clèves."

"I heard them from your own lips, Madame."
And he began to tell how he had come
To Coulommiers, had been in the pavilion

And, from the outer room, had seen
Her with her husband in the avenue
And, forced to hide, had listened when they entered.


"I understand at last then how you knew,
On that occasion with Mme la Dauphine,
So much of what she had heard,
                      since you yourself
Divulged it."
              M. de Nemours
Explained how this had come about; he had,
He said, been rash and overwhelmed by feeling,
And had confided in the Vidame only
The wonder and the fact, but named no-one.


"Make no excuse," said Mme de Clèves.
"I have long since forgiven you without
The need for explanation. Yet, because
You have learnt from my lips the revelation
Which I had meant to hide from you for ever,
I confess
        that you aroused in me a state
Of feelings such as I knew nothing of
Before I saw you. I was taken by
Surprise, I found myself — I lost myself —
In a strange confusion.
                I make this confession now
With no great sense of shame since, as you have seen,
My conduct was not led by my emotions."


"Can such manna fall from your lips
And you not know that I must die of joy
Here at your feet?"
               She smiled. "And yet

I have only said what you already knew."

"But ah! the difference, Madame, between
Discovering such things by chance and, now,
Your willingness that I should know."

She said, "I understand.
And it is true I wanted you to know
And found the telling sweet.
                              But my confession
Will have not the slightest consequence
Since I must follow that austere path
Which duty still imposes on me."

"Madame," replied M. de Nemours,
"No duty ties your hands now. You are free."

Gravely she smiled and said,
                              "My duty now forbids
Such freedoms and such thoughts of anyone —
Not least of you —
For reasons of which you are unaware."

"I am perhaps aware of them, Madame;
They are not genuine. And I have grounds
To think M. de Clèves assumed that I
Was happier than I was,
                              believing as he did
That you approved the excesses of my passion."

"Enough!
        I cannot bear to think about
Those latest visits to Coulommiers.
The painful truth is that you are the cause

Of M. de Clèves' death,
                              no less than if he had
Died at your hands. Imagine, if you will,
The consequences for my duty, had
You put your quarrel to the ultimate test
And you had killed him in a duel."


"Ah! Madame," cried M. de Nemours,
                                        "would you allow
Such phantom and delusory duty to prevent
My happiness?  Will vain and groundless fancy
Stand before my hopes of marrying you,
The woman who of all women is
Most worthy of esteem, in whom I see
The qualities of mistress and of wife
Combined supremely?
                              Can it be
That I have glimpsed such bliss, only to see
You interpose these obstacles which seem
No more than fear of happiness?"


"I must speak openly, and set aside
Discretion and evasiveness,
The reticence which I might otherwise
Assume with you.
                              For, as implacable
And insurmountable as seem the demands
Of duty, there are other obstacles
No less oppressive. I confess
My fears quite freely to you:
The certainty that one day this bright love
You feel for me will die. That certainty
Seems so appalling that I could not face
So much unhappiness.

I know the world
Might see that we are free and not find blame
In us, were we to bind ourselves for life.
But can man's passion last when he is bound
For ever?  Could I expect a miracle?
If not, could I resign myself
To that eventual, inevitable decline?
I think M. de Clèves may well have been
The one exception to this rule. Perhaps
His passion only lasted when he found
No answering passion in his wife. But I fear
I could not guarantee yours in this way.
Indeed I fear your constancy
Has been sustained by constant obstacles."

"Ah!  Madame," exclaimed M. de Nemours,
"I must protest. This is unjust. You are
No longer bound by arduous duty, and
Your fears on my account are quite unfounded — "

"And yet I cannot fail to recognise
That you were born susceptible to love,
With all the qualities required to prosper
In its lists. You have already had
A number of attachments, passionate
And serious; you would have others.
I should see you drawn to other women
As you were drawn to me. I should be wounded.
Already I was struck by jealousy
When first I saw Mme de Thémines' letter,
Thinking it addressed to you.
And even were I able to endure
The misery of thinking you in love
With every woman who was moved by you

And met your gaze, there is the suffering
Of hearing M. de Clèves reproaching me.
I beg you to believe I cannot change.
I must continue in my present state
And stand by my resolve
                                        not to abandon it."


M. de Nemours cried out:
"But do you think you can succeed?  Can you
Hold firm against a man who worships you
And who is fortunate in having won your heart?
It is harder than you think, Madame, to resist
Someone who both attracts and loves you.
                                                        So far
You have succeeded, thanks to a virtue quite
Unparalleled in its austerity.
But now your virtue need not be opposed
To your feelings, and I hope
That you will follow these in spite of yourself."


"I am aware that nothing is more difficult
Than what I seek to do.
                                I would put little faith
In my own powers or those of solemn duty
Were they not underpinned by self-interest,
Namely, the need for some tranquillity of mind.


Of course tranquillity is difficult.
For just as I can never overcome
My scruples, equally I cannot quell
My attraction to you.
                                Thus I intend
To remove myself entirely from your sight,
However violent the pain

Of separation.
                    And I implore you,
By all the power I have to influence you,
Never to seek the opportunity
To see or speak to me."

M. de Nemours fell at her feet,
                              surrendering himself
Entirely to the weight of hope scattered like ash,
Long galleries and towers of gold
                              turned into lead.
His desperate words and tears revealed to her
A love tender and ardent.
                    She herself
Was not insensible. Through brimming tears
She said,
          "Why must I be obliged
To blame you for M. de Clèves' death?
Why could I not have met you after it,
Or when I was still free, when fate had not
Yet placed insuperable obstacles between us?"

"Madame, there is no obstacle.
You alone stand in the way of happiness.
You alone have made
A law which reason never could impose."

"It is true," she said, "that I have sacrificed
My happiness to a duty which exists
In my imagination."
She looked away with vague uncertainty
Beyond M. de Nemours. "Wait and see
What time may bring. M. de Clèves has still
So recently died. I can see nothing plainly.

Meanwhile be assured that you have won the heart
Of one who never would have loved
Had she not known you,
                          and do not doubt
My feelings will not change."


She now was pale and drawn
As one who waits all night outside the room
Of someone in his final hours.
                          She said,
"Farewell.
            This conversation now makes me ashamed.
Tell the Vidame all that we have said."


She found her uncle in the next room.
He saw her deep distress; he did not speak
But took her gently to her carriage.
                          Then he returned.
M. de Nemours, it seemed, was filled with joy
And grief and wonder and confusion, all
Contending. Fear and hope divided him.
The Vidame heard in fragments the account
Of all Mme de Clèves had said.
                          He tried
To give advice and offer hope. He thought
That possibly Mme de Clèves' resolve
Might not endure. But, equally, he thought
Nemours should now obey her and resist
The overwhelming wish to speak to her.


M. de Nemours reluctantly agreed.
He would accompany the King,
                          and leave
Without revisiting the dazzling room

From which he had observed her.

                                 But he plied
The Vidame with messages, instructions, thoughts,
Provisions, reasons, arguments, which might
Persuade Mme de Clèves.

                         At length he left,
But it was far into the night before
The Vidame was left in peace.

For Mme de Clèves peace too was difficult.
To have allowed someone
As she had never done before, to plead
His love for her, to say that she loved him —
She was amazed, she scarcely recognised
Herself. She felt regret, she felt delight,
The arguments against her happiness
She constantly rehearsed, and sought to find
Some flaw in them. She felt that she had voiced
Too strongly to M. de Nemours these bonds.
She constantly was drawn back to the charm
Of love and its confession. Equally
She bore the iron weight of those constraints
And felt the flower crushed against the wheel.
She reached at last some slight degree of calm
By thinking that she need not yet decide.

But when the Vidame next spoke to her and urged
Persuasively the merits of Nemours,
She said that she was quite resolved to stay
In her present state; she made him see the power
That duty exercised; she would not hear
Of counter argument, and the Vidame
Could see his best hopes for Nemours begin
To wither like a vine in winter frost.

The two men left the following day.

They joined the King.

M. de Nemours prevailed upon the Vidame
To write a letter to Mme de Clèves
And speak of him. A second letter bore
A brief addition in Nemours' own hand.
Mme de Clèves, fearing the accidents
Which letters can entail,
Sent word that she would not receive
His letters if they dwelt on M. de Nemours.
Even Nemours himself then begged his friend
To mention him no more.

The court now travelled with the Queen of Spain
As far as Poitou.

During these long days
Mme de Clèves was much alone. In time,
As M. de Nemours, and everything that might
Remind her of him, grew remote, she found
The present slowly filling like a pool
With memories of M. de Clèves; she felt
Once more the deadening calm of duty's claims
Which argued against marrying Nemours.

They seemed increasingly entwined with that
Most insurmountable reason, peace of mind:
The eventual cooling of M. de Nemours
Towards her, and the ills of jealousy,
Which she believed inevitable in marriage,
Loomed as a warning.

Yet she saw also
That, were she to see him still,
She could not possibly resist
The man who loved her and whom she too loved

When neither virtue nor decorum intervened.

In consequence, two days before the court
Returned, she set out on a long journey
To spend time at a large estate of hers
In the Pyrenees,
                    where distance, altitude
And the rigours of the journey might provide
Some first line of defence.
                              She left a letter
For the Vidame in which she begged that no-one
Seek news of her or write to her.

M. de Nemours suffered at the thought
Of such an absence — as if all the world
Were gathered up and taken from his arms
Into the Pyrenees.
                    His suffering soon increased:
Word reached the court that at this journey's end
So far from court, she fell
Into a violent illness.
                    M. de Nemours
Was inconsolable.
                    The Vidame had difficulty
Restraining him from a damaging display
Of public grief,
                    and scarcely could prevent
His setting out at once in search of news.

The Vidame, as both her uncle and her friend,
Was able to send messengers.
                              At length they heard
That she was not in peril of her life
But lingered in a malady

Which offered little hope of full recovery.

This long, close view of death
Mme de Clèves
Held to her like a small, fragrant bouquet,
And over its stellated hedge
She saw this life with different eyes.

The imminence of death
Encouraged the detachment she had sought
And, as her illness tightened like a vine,
The habit of detachment was ingrained.

But even so, on certain days,
                           days when
That illness loosened its strong grasp,
                                she found
M. de Nemours still living in her heart.
Then she would summon all the arguments
Which had defended her against his power
And, in a now familiar combat, win
A difficult truce.

Her state of health which still was very weak
Helped her preserve this distance from the world
Of passion,
             but having learned the power of chance events
Over the strictest resolutions, she
Was wary of returning to a place
Frequented by the man whom she had loved.

Under the pretext of a change of air
She went into a convent's cloistered shade
Although without abandoning for ever

The company of the court.

The Duc de Nemours heard of this change. At once
He sensed the end of hope. And yet he sought
In every way to gain Mme de Clèves' return.
He asked the Queen to write, he asked
The Vidame to write, he sent the Vidame in person.
All was in vain.
                        The Vidame had seen her, and,
Although she did not say her cloistered life
Was final and definitive, he felt
That she would never return.
                        M. de Nemours
At last went there himself with the excuse
Of taking the waters.
                        She was much disturbed
To hear of his arrival.
                        In the whitewashed hall
He waited. Then an older woman came
And spoke to him, a candle's shuffling beam
In place of that consuming radiance —
Which he was not to see again.
                        He heard:
She begged him not to find it strange
If she did not expose herself to risk
In seeing him.
                        She wished to make it clear
That finding duty and her peace of mind
Irreconcilable with her desire
                        to be with him,
All other aspects of this world had seemed
So much a matter of indifference,
She had renounced them, and might hope
That he could find so great a peace.

M. de Nemours in grief and anguish begged
A hundred times that this calm woman go
Once more to Mme de Clèves
And prevail on her to let him speak to her.
He sensed behind closed doors the captive light.
But she said softly that Mme de Clèves
Forbade her bringing messages from him
Or even telling her what had been said.

The corridors were adamant.
He was obliged to leave, shrouded with grief,
As only a man could be who now had lost
The woman whom he loved more violently
Than any man loved in the world.
                               And yet
He still did not give up, but tried each day
To think of ways to make her change her mind,
Until, when years had poured their cooling stream
On pain and passion, he became resigned.
She spent part of each year at home
But in profound retreat, the rest within
The cool shade of the convent walls.
Her life, which was quite short,
Was seen as virtuous and inimitable.

www.ingramcontent.com/pod-product-compliance
Lightning Source LLC
Chambersburg PA
CBHW030942090426
42737CB00007B/511